Key Considerations
For Irregular Security Forces
In Counterinsurgency

A thesis presented to the Faculty of the U.S. Army
Command and General Staff College

By

ROBERT L. GREEN, MAJOR, U.S. ARMY
B.A., University of Minnesota, Minneapolis, Minnesota

Fort Leavenworth, Kansas
2011-01

Abstract
Key Considerations For Irregular Security Forces
In Counterinsurgency

By Robert L. Green

Counterinsurgents have raised and employed irregular security forces in many campaigns over the last century. Irregular security forces are indigenous forces, not part of the regular police or military organizations of the host nation, that are recruited locally to provide a basic level of security in a given area. Irregular security forces, when used in conjunction with all other available capabilities, contribute to, but do not in and of themselves, ensure success. While irregular security forces can be effective in conducting local security, intelligence gathering, surveillance and other tasks in their home areas, tasks that may prove more difficult for regular security forces, irregular forces are no silver bullet to achieving success. Counterinsurgency is a struggle for the support of the population against an active and thinking enemy and therefore, there are no hard and fast rules. Several counterinsurgency scholars and theorists do, however, agree on several key principles that can aid counterinsurgents in prosecuting their campaigns successfully. This paper seeks to add to the body of knowledge by examining the key aspects that counterinsurgents should take into account when considering raising an irregular security force.

Acknowledgments

This thesis represents the support of my family, the leadership of past mentors, the support of the college, and the guidance of Dr. Daniel Marston. I and the other scholars are indebted to the Army for the opportunity this program provided. Many people contributed their personal time and recollections to our program, which was of great benefit to our research, and personally a great honor. I would like to thank in particular the men of the Special Air Service and the Sultan's Armed Forces who shared their experiences in Dhofar so many years ago. I would also like to thank Balliol College at Oxford for hosting us and allowing us the use of their facilities for part of our research.

Objectives of the Art of War Scholars Program

The Art of War Scholars Program is a laboratory for critical thinking. It offers a select group of students a range of accelerated, academically rigorous graduate level courses that promote analysis, stimulate the desire for life-long learning, and reinforce academic research skills. Art of War graduates will not be satisfied with facile arguments; they understand the complexities inherent in almost any endeavor and develop the tools and fortitude to confront such complexities, analyze challenges, and independently seek nuanced solutions in the face of those who would opt for cruder alternatives. Through the pursuit of these outcomes, the Art of War Scholars Program seeks to improve and deepen professional military education.

The Art of War Program places contemporary operations (such as those in Iraq and Afghanistan) in a historical framework by examining earlier military campaigns. Case studies and readings have been selected to show the consistent level of complexity posed by military campaigns throughout the modern era. Coursework emphasizes the importance of understanding previous engagements in order to formulate policy and doctrinal response to current and future campaigns.

One unintended consequence of military history education is the phenomenon of commanders and policy makers "cherry picking" history—that is, pointing to isolated examples from past campaigns to bolster a particular position in a debate, without a comprehensive understanding of the context in which such incidents occurred. This trend of oversimplification leaves many historians wary of introducing these topics into broader, more general discussion. The Art of War program seeks to avoid this pitfall by a thorough examination of context. As one former student stated: "The insights gained have left me with more questions than answers but have increased my ability to understand greater complexities of war rather than the rhetorical narrative that accompanies cursory study of any topic."

Professor Michael Howard, writing "The Use and Abuse of Military History" in 1961, proposed a framework for educating military officers in the art of war that remains unmatched in its clarity, simplicity, and totality. The Art of War program endeavors to model his plan:

Three general rules of study must therefore be borne in mind by the officer who studies military history as a guide to his profession and who wishes to avoid pitfalls. First, he must study in **width**. He must observe the way in which warfare has developed over a long historical period. Only by seeing what does change can one deduce what does not; and as much as can be learnt from the great discontinuities of military history as from the apparent similarities of the techniques employed by the great captains through the ages....Next he must study in **depth**. He should take a single campaign and explore it thoroughly, not simply from official histories, but from memoirs, letters, diaries. . . until the tidy outlines dissolve and he catches a glimpse of the confusion and horror of real experience... and, lastly, he must study in **context**. Campaigns and battles are not like games of chess or football matches, conducted in total detachment from their environment according to strictly defined rules. Wars are not tactical exercises writ large. They are...conflicts of societies, and they can be fully understood only if one understands the nature of the society fighting them. The roots of victory and defeat often have to be sought far from the battlefield, in political, social, and economic factors which explain why armies are constituted as they are, and why their leaders conduct them in the way they do....

It must not be forgotten that the true use of history, military or civil... is not to make men clever for the next time; it is to make them wise forever.

Gordon B. Davis, Jr.   Daniel Marston
Brigadier General, US Army   DPhil (Oxon) FRHistS
Deputy Commanding General   Ike Skelton Distinguished Chair
CAC LD&E   in the Art of War
                              US Army Command & General
                              Staff College

Table of Contents

GLOSSARY

AFM	Army Field Manual
ANM	Arab Nationalist Movement
AQI	Al Qaeda in Iraq
BATT	British Army Training Team
CAP	Combined Action Platoon
CENTCOM	U.S. Central Command
CSAF	Commander, Sultan's Armed Forces
DCA	Dhofar Charitable Association
DLF	Dhofar Liberation Front
MNSTC-I	Multi-National Security Transition Command-Iraq
NATO	North Atlantic Treaty Alliance
OMLT	Operational Mentoring and Liaison Team
OPLAN	Operations Plan
PFLOAG	Popular Front for the Liberation of the Occupied Arabian Gulf
PLA	People's Liberation Army
SAF	Sultan of Oman's Armed Forces
SAS	Special Air Service

Chapter 1
Introduction

Mankind has waged insurgencies and counterinsurgencies throughout history.[1] Despite the large volume of material available for the study of these forms of conflict, there yet remains a great deal of myth and confusion surrounding insurgency and counterinsurgency. Modern western militaries largely neglected the study of counterinsurgency prior to the attacks on the United States on 11 September 2001. Stung by the loss in Vietnam, the US military chose to minimize counterinsurgency[2] and focused on the conventional warfare which it preferred and was better trained, organized, and equipped to conduct.

This choice was not merely academic, but impacted the way the Army trained, procured equipment, educated its leaders, and prepared for war. As Jonathan M. House wrote in *Combined Arms Warfare in the Twentieth Century*, "To meet the challenge of the wars of national liberation, Western armies had two choices – they could attempt to adapt their conventional forces to a style of war for which they were not intended, or they could neglect the development of new generations of armored weapons in favor of a renewed interest in light infantry forces."[3] Should the United States expend the bulk of its resources to prepare its forces to win proxy wars of insurgency and counterinsurgency, or should it remain prepared to win the less likely but more serious conventional conflict with the Soviet Union? After Vietnam the choice was clear, and counterinsurgency was mostly discarded by the conventional force as a task for Special Forces.[4]

As the United States focused more on the possible conventional fight between the North Atlantic Treaty Alliance (NATO) and the Soviet-backed Warsaw Pact, American strategy and doctrine envisaged a battle against numerically superior enemy forces[5] which required a defensive posture reliant more on firepower than maneuver.[6] In order to increase the odds of survival against a numerically superior enemy, American military leaders pressed for weapons systems with greater precision in an attempt to improve the Army's odds on the battlefield.[7]

While precision weapons provide certain advantages, reliance upon them and idealistic overestimation of their capabilities supported false impressions of the true capabilities of a force. The decisive defeat of Saddam Hussein's forces in the 1991 Gulf War bolstered and propelled the faith in technological silver bullets to ensure dominance in future armed conflict.[8] As Lieutenant Colonel H.R. McMaster wrote in his War College research paper, "The prevailing explanation for victory in the Gulf War – technological superiority – led many to believe that America had already generated or now had the opportunity to craft a "revolution in military affairs" or RMA."[9]

If technology can provide silver bullets, all that remains is to determine what kind of threat must be eliminated. This leads to over-categorization of war as a necessary step in the process to develop silver-bullet solutions.[10] As the former Army Chief of Staff, General George Casey, wrote in his October 2009 article in *ARMY* magazine, "Formerly, we could differentiate and categorize threats as conventional or unconventional; regular or irregular; high intensity or low intensity; traditional, terrorist or criminal. Such categorization was useful because each categorized threat had an associated counter."[11] The tendency to try to categorize warfare creates confusion, a muddled lexicon of catch-phrases, and leads to the search for a silver bullet as the "associated counter" to each type of threat.

The United States Army is not alone in its over-categorization of war. Frank Kitson[12] commented on the confusion created by the use of several different terms used to describe basically the same type of conflict (e.g. "Civil Disturbance, Insurgency, Guerilla Warfare, Subversion, Terrorism").[13] Despite the fact that the armies of the US and UK have fought shoulder-to-shoulder in Iraq and Afghanistan for nearly a decade, and as a result each has revised its counterinsurgency doctrine with each manual citing Kitson's works, each force has similar but distinct definitions for counterinsurgency and insurgency.

The United States Army and Marine Corps field manual on counterinsurgency, FM 3-24, defines counterinsurgency as "Those military, paramilitary, political, economic, psychological, and civic actions taken by a government to defeat insurgency."[14] The British counterinsurgency manual, Army Field Manual (AFM) Volume 1:10 (2010), defines counterinsurgency as "Those military, law enforcement, political, economic, psychological and civic actions taken to defeat insurgency while addressing the root causes."[15] Counterinsurgency therefore is reactionary towards insurgency. The important question now becomes what are they countering? What is insurgency?

FM 3-24 defines insurgency as "An organized movement aimed at the overthrow of a constituted government through the use of subversion and armed conflict."[16] The British AFM 1:10 defines insurgency as "An organized, violent subversion used to effect or prevent political control, as a challenge to established authority."[17] US and UK doctrine agree at least that insurgencies include violence and subversion.

King's College London, professor and author John Mackinlay's definition of insurgency, found in his book, *The Insurgent Archipelago*, agrees with the US and UK Army field manuals:

> [G]roups which used bombing, assassination, hostage-taking and similar acts, but failed to combine these acts with a broader subversive campaign, quickly found themselves fastened in a cycle of violence that seldom succeeded in gaining the sympathy of a wider population; they could therefore be correctly regarded

as terrorists. But a movement which in addition to committing acts of terrorism also had a political strategy to subvert the population to such an extent that it attracted a reciprocating political response from the government, amounted to something more than terrorism. By successfully involving a substantial element of the population they raised the game from terrorism to insurgency.[18]

According to Mackinlay, insurgency includes both subversion and violence. David Kilcullen, a fellow contemporary author and counterinsurgency adviser, offers this definition of insurgency in his book, *Counterinsurgency*: "...an insurgency is an organized, protracted politico-military struggle designed to weaken the control and legitimacy of an established government, or occupying power, or other political authority while increasing insurgent control."[19] While Kilcullen's definition doesn't address the violence and subversion elements as directly as the definitions found in the manuals, one can assume that an organized struggle combining political and military components included both subversion and violence.

While the field manuals and these two authors generally agree that insurgency is the combination of subversion and violence, well-known counterinsurgency theorists of the Cold War[20] era were not so uniform in their definitions of insurgency. For example, Frank Kitson separated subversion from insurgency.

> Subversion, then, will be held to mean all illegal measures short of the use of armed force taken by one section of the people of a country to overthrow those governing the country at the time, or to force them to do things which they do not want to do. Insurgency will be held to cover the use of armed force by a section of the people against the government for the purposes mentioned above.[21]

Robert Thompson[22] also saw a distinction between subversion and insurgency, but placed them in order as a natural progression of conflict.

> The stage has been reached when the communists are ready for, but still not quite committed to, open insurgency. The main prong of their attack, subversion supported by selective terrorism, has reached a point at which they have to decide whether they can bring the government down by this means alone, or whether they will have to use the second prong of their attack, "armed struggle." Insurgency is a measure both of the success and of the failure of subversion.[23]

According to Thompson, insurgency is the openly violent stage which follows subversion but only when subversion alone fails to bring down the government.

David Galula's[24] definition of insurgency did not use terms such as subversion or violence but dealt more with the process of overthrowing authority.[25] "On the other hand, an insurgency is a protracted struggle conducted methodically, step by step, in order to attain specific intermediate objectives leading finally to the overthrow of the existing order."[26] While Galula's definition did not directly address violence, terrorism, or subversion, he did describe the "cold" and "hot" phases of the insurgent's campaign which emphasize subversion and violence respectively.[27] Perhaps Galula's more general definition was due to the fact that his only counterinsurgency experience at the time he wrote his book was as a French tactical level commander during the Algerian War of Independence.

Roger Trinquier, another commander of French troops during the Algerian War of Independence, saw insurgency as a new form of warfare and called it modern warfare.[28] "Warfare is now an interlocking system of actions – political, economic, psychological, military – that aims at the overthrow of the established authority in a country and its replacement by another regime."[29] Perhaps, such as with Galula, Trinquier was commenting more broadly on nature of armed conflict in the modern era.

Trinquier was trying to articulate his vision of the future of armed conflict so that his nation could better prepare, hopefully avoiding another defeat. As Carl von Clausewitz famously advised,

> As the first, the supreme, the most far reaching act of judgment that the statesman and commander have to make is to establish the kind of war on which they are embarking, neither mistaking it for, nor trying to turn it into something that is alien to its nature. This is the first of all strategic questions and the most comprehensive.[30]

Although it is important to understand the nature of the conflict, it is equally important to recognize that warfare is characterized by uncertainty. As H. R. McMaster wrote in an article regarding the character of conflict, "Indeed, leaders must recognize that war on land will remain fundamentally in the realm of uncertainty due to the human, psychological, political and cultural dimensions of conflict as well as the immanent interaction with adversaries able to use terrain, intermingle with the population, and adopt countermeasures to technological capabilities."[31] This brings us back to the former Army Chief of Staff's comment regarding categorizing threats in order to develop appropriate counters. Superficially studying a campaign to identify one aspect or capability as the counter to the threat causes one to take a narrow view of conflict. After identifying the silver bullet, one then attempts to replicate not only the solution to the last conflict, but also the very nature of the last conflict as a comfortable problem frame.

The treatment of the Malayan Emergency in FM 3-24 provides an interesting example of the need for context. According to the manual, police reform and development were the keys to victory in the campaign. "The Malaya insurgency provides lessons applicable to combating any insurgency. Manpower is not enough; well-trained and well-disciplined forces are required. The Malayan example also illustrates the central role that police play in counterinsurgency operations."[32] The first sentence in the quote above would be true if it began with, "Once the context of the campaign is understood. . ." The second sentence is fairly obvious. Not until the third sentence do we begin to see the problem of looking for the silver bullet in a successful campaign. This broad generalization regarding the central role of police in successful counterinsurgency campaigns is not true. For example, police were not a major factor in the successful counterinsurgency campaign in Dhofar.[33]

The simple term "police" itself is vague. Were the authors referring to the Home Guards who were a form of police auxiliaries, the local uniformed police who handled minor crime and dealt with law and order issues in population centers, or the Police Field Force (police jungle squads) which conducted counter-guerrilla operations?[34] Additionally, the police were only one part of the security forces which were only one element of the campaign strategy.[35] Without exploring the details of the Malayan Emergency, it would be easy for one reading FM 3-24 to conclude that a successful counterinsurgency strategy must include indigenous police forces as its centerpiece, or as the "associated counter" to the insurgent threat.

The value of FM 3-24 and AFM 1:10 is in their discussion of general principles of counterinsurgency warfare.[36] While some principles included in these manuals were the result of examinations of the conflicts in Iraq and Afghanistan, most of the principles were developed by many of the authors mentioned thus far (e.g. Galula, Thompson, and Kitson). Because these past authors, and some modern ones, developed their principles based on an in-depth examination of various counterinsurgency campaigns, they have proven to be of value in understanding the nature of counterinsurgency operations. Indeed, most modern theorists use many of the same principles derived from the study of the last 200 years of counterinsurgency experience.

Unlike strategists who seek victory through, and advocate for, silver bullets (e.g. advanced command and control networks and information dominance[37]), classic counterinsurgency theorists such as Thompson, Kitson, and Galula acknowledge the unpredictable nature of conflict. These theorists describe what worked in specific campaigns and how the general principles of those successful components could apply without attempting to portray their ideas as guarantees of success. A brief discussion of the key principles developed by classic and modern counterinsurgency authors follows.

Galula's most influential contributions to the study and practice of counterinsurgency were the importance of protecting the population, and the primacy of political power over military power.[38] In his own words,

> Destroying or expelling from an area the main body of the guerrilla forces, preventing their return, installing garrisons to protect the population, tracking the guerrilla remnants–these are predominantly military operations.[39]

> That the political power is the undisputed boss is a matter of both principle and practicality. What is at stake is the country's political regime, and to defend it is a political affair. Even if this requires military action, the action is constantly directed toward a political goal. Essential though it is, the military action is secondary to the political one, its primary purpose being to afford the political power enough freedom to work safely with the population.[40]

Galula further stated that the political and military aspects of the counterinsurgency campaign are multiplied and not added to reach a product and not a sum, and that if any of the factors is zero, the product, or results of the campaign, will also be zero.[41]

In addition to these tenets, Galula offered four laws. The first law stated that the support of the population is as necessary for the counterinsurgent as for the insurgent.[42] His second law stated that support is gained through an active minority, which requires those supporting the counterinsurgents to assist in gaining the support of the neutral minority against the minority which supports the insurgents.[43] Galula's third law cautioned that support from the population is conditional based on the perception of the counterinsurgents' strength, will and capability to win, and demonstrated success against the insurgents.[44] Galula's fourth law advised against diluting efforts and resources across the entire area of operations but rather concentrating them area by area to relieve the population and convince them of the counterinsurgents' viability.[45]

Thompson also developed a set of five principles to guide future counterinsurgents based on his experiences in various campaigns. As with Galula, Thompson emphasized the role of politics in counterinsurgency as well as the importance of protecting the population while also advocating for a clear political aim and plan for the campaign.[46] As the predecessor to the contemporary term "clear, hold, build," Thompson coined the term "clear and hold" as part of his four stage operational concept:[47]

> For "clear" operations the ... area itself should be selected as an extension of an area already securely held, and should first be subjected to an intense intelligence effort before any operations start…the first essential is to saturate it with joint military and police forces. This will force the insurgent units

either to disperse within the area or possibly to withdraw to neighbouring areas still under their control or disputed. The government's forces should then be so deployed as to make it impossible for the insurgent forces to reconcentrate within the area or to re-infiltrate from outside. Clear operations will, however, be a waste of time unless the government is ready to follow them up immediately with "hold" operations. ... The objects of a hold operation are to restore government authority in the area and to establish a firm security framework. ... This hold period of operations inevitably takes a considerable time. ... It never really ends.[48]

Thompson's concept was put to good use in the Iraqi city of Tal Afar in 2005 by the 3d Armored Cavalry Regiment[49] whose commander was well versed in the works of Galula, Thompson, and Kitson.[50]

The final classic theorist discussed is Frank Kitson, who wrote *Low Intensity Operations: Subversion, Insurgency and Peacekeeping* that encapsulated his experiences in campaigns in Malaya, Kenya, and Cyprus. While Kitson provided a detailed and comprehensive examination of counterinsurgency, his most profound contribution centered on intelligence collection. According to General Sir Michael Carver,[51] "The necessity for the intimate integration of intelligence and operations is his most important lesson and the one least appreciated by the conventional soldier."[52] As noted in *Counterinsurgency in Modern Warfare*, "More than any other theorist, he explained the importance and methods of intelligence collection and training. Indeed, he is the first to articulate intelligence collection as key to success, rather than assuming it to be an unstated and integral aspect of other principles."[53]

Kitson regarded intelligence as consisting of two main functions – collection of background information, and development of actionable intelligence.[54] The whole purpose of these intelligence functions was to put troops in contact with the insurgents.[55] Kitson offered, "To over-simplify the full process it could be said that it is the responsibility of the intelligence organization to produce background information and that it is then up to operational commanders to develop it to the extent necessary for their men to make contact with the enemy, using their own resources."[56]

Frank Kitson placed a great deal of emphasis on the role of the commander in the intelligence function of a counterinsurgency campaign. He acknowledged the fact that fulfilling this role would require a great deal of the commander's time and focus.[57] Kitson justified commanders' devotion of time and energy to the intelligence function against criticism that acting in this manner would cause commanders to neglect the other duties associated with command.

But the point has already been made that the main problem in fighting insurgents lies in finding them ...a tactical commander should concentrate on it, and in any case the business cannot be delegated, because the process of absorbing the background information and making plans for the use of the troops based on it is inseparable from the function of command. Either the commander does it or it is not done at all.[58]

Kitson concluded his 200-plus page book on counterinsurgency by cautioning the reader that, "Although such a cursory examination can not be expected to lead to any fundamental conclusions, it might at least serve to provide a stepping stone for a further study."[59] This type of humility underscores the classic counterinsurgency theorists' understanding that there are no associated counters to insurgency, only general principles which emerge only after in-depth examination of multiple conflicts.

David Kilcullen continued this sentiment, stating, "there are no standard templates or universal solutions in counterinsurgency. Fundamentals and principles exist, but they require judgment in application, and there is no substitute for studying the environment in detail, developing locally tailored solutions, and being prepared to adjust them in an agile way as the situation develops."[60] Kilcullen offered his views in the form of "Twenty-Eight Articles,"[61] a distillation of his observations of company-level counterinsurgency best practices.[62]

Another set of fourteen counterinsurgency fundamentals offered by contemporary authors is included in the introduction of *Counterinsurgency in Modern Warfare*.[63] Key among these fundamentals are "Comprehension of existing history and doctrine.... Adaptation to local situations and learning from mistakes. ... Population security ... and Raise, mentor, and fight alongside host nation forces."[64] Developed from an examination of selected counterinsurgency campaigns from 1898 to present, and ongoing campaigns in Iraq and Afghanistan, the list of fundamentals "attempts to capture some of the elements which are present in successful COIN campaigns."[65] As with Kitson and Kilcullen, the authors emphasize the complex nature of counterinsurgency operations which confounds any attempts to rely on a "silver bullet" solution.[66]

Despite the long period of neglect in the US military's study of counterinsurgency, the results of past campaigns have once again emerged to be studied. This is evident in the first revision of US Army and Marine Corps counterinsurgency doctrine in decades as well as a thorough revision of the UK Army's counterinsurgency doctrine. Additional evidence includes the guidance issued by commanders at the highest level in the ongoing war in Afghanistan such as the following from the former senior US commander in Afghanistan, General Stanley McCrystal:

1. Protect and Partner with the People.

2. Conduct a Comprehensive Counterinsurgency Campaign.

3. Understand the Environment.

4. Ensure Values Underpin our Effort.

5. Listen Closely—Speak Clearly.

6. Act as One Team.

7. Constantly Adapt.

8. Act with Courage and Resolve.[67]

This guidance reflects many of the principles, rules, and themes identified by past and contemporary students of counterinsurgency.

Recognition of the need to discard unrealistic aspirations of "silver bullets" to counter security threats now resides in the office of the senior US Army officer, newly appointed Army Chief of Staff General Martin E. Dempsey. During a speech on 25 February 2010, General Dempsey said:

> Technology will never deliver everything we need to know about our adversaries. Army forces must first strive to understand the situation in depth, width and context, then develop the situation through action, adjusting the approach over time as needed. To understand our enemies' capabilities, intentions, morale and level of support among the civilian population, we have to think, act, learn and then adapt.[68]

Despite General Dempsey's comments and guidance issued by senior commanders engaged in counterinsurgency operations, there remains a tendency to attempt to extrapolate solutions developed at lower levels across the operational area in a "cookie-cutter" manner. This may be due in part to intense pressure to produce results, or a fundamental lack of understanding of the principles of counterinsurgency described thus far. It may also stem from thinking such as that expressed by Trinquier which advocated for a single hand guiding the ship:

> The struggle against the guerrilla is not, as one might suppose, a war of lieutenants and captains. The number of troops that must be put into action, the vast areas over which they will be led to do battle, the necessity of coordinating diverse actions over these vast areas, the politico-military measures to be taken regarding the populace, the necessarily close cooperation with various branches of the civil administration – all this requires that operations against the guerrilla be conducted according to a plan, established at a very high command level.[69]

Trinquier's comment has merit, especially in a campaign lacking much diversity across the operational area (e.g. ethnic, tribal, political, religious). In more complex environments such as Afghanistan and Iraq, Trinquier's vision of centralized control becomes more difficult as the conditions change dramatically from one valley to another, indeed from one neighborhood to the next. As stated in the 2009 Army Capstone Concept, "The uniqueness of local conditions and uncertainty associated with the interaction of Army forces with the enemy and complex environments will confound efforts to develop an aggregated common operational picture as a basis for centralized decision making or control of forces."[70]

The attempt to replicate the Al Anbar Awakening[71] through the Sons of Iraq[72] was an example of this ongoing issue. In Al Anbar province, a predominantly Sunni area of Iraq, the traditional leaders and the people of the resident tribes saw Al Qaeda as the greater evil over the American troops and sought assistance in ousting Al Qaeda.[73] It signaled a tectonic shift in the will of the people of Al Anbar province. Unlike the Anbar Awakening, the Sons of Iraq program sought to replicate the product of the Awakening, irregular forces securing their areas against Al Qaeda activity and influence, without the unity of the communities to bind them together and support them.

What led U.S. senior commanders to believe such a shallow replication of events in Al Anbar could work? Perhaps the true reasons for the shift in Sunni attitude in Al Anbar were misunderstood. One side of the debate discussed by Najim al Jabouri, a former Iraqi Army and Iraqi Police officer, and former mayor of Tal Afar, believed that the Anbar Awakening was a result of successful coalition operations resulting in the confidence of the people. "Contrary to a growing U.S. narrative about the Sunni Awakening being mainly the fruit of U.S. counterinsurgency tactics, in Ramadi having the U.S. forces in the neighborhoods was not what made the people feel safe. They felt safe when their men could join the police force and secure their areas by themselves."[74]

Certainly it appears that the Sons of Iraq, in conjunction with other efforts during the period of the Surge, had a positive impact and contributed to the success of the campaign.[75] If nothing else, the Sons of Iraq initiative tied local Iraqis and their families to the US-led coalition and the Iraqi government while creating a local security force able to hold cleared areas against re-infiltration of insurgents.[76] The fact that a locally raised security force was effective in supporting the government against insurgents is not surprising given the examination of classic and modern counterinsurgency theorists who all agree such forces are vital to success.

Raising conventional security forces is fairly straightforward forward but takes a long time and often fails to produce forces able to gather intelligence critical in counterinsurgency operations. As author James Corum concluded in *Training Indigenous Forces in Counterinsurgency: A Tale of Two Insurgencies*, regarding counterinsurgency campaigns in Malaya and Cyprus,

> What determined government success or failure in counterguerrilla operations was not force size or firepower,

but intelligence. … In counterinsurgency campaigns, military units and special police strike units, such as the police jungle companies in Malaya, are routinely shifted around to different sectors, according to the needs of the moment, while police remain on the ground dealing with civilians on a daily basis and, hopefully, building a detailed intelligence picture of the insurgent strength, organization, and support in each local sector. Effective counterinsurgency relies on good human intelligence, and no military unit can match a good police unit in developing an accurate human intelligence picture of their area of operations.[77]

The Sons of Iraq were not police though many among them aspired to one day join the police.[78] The Sons of Iraq shared many characteristics with the police forces described by Corum as they were from the community in which they operated, were not employed outside of their communities,[79] and were therefore able to provide additional intelligence. As Greg Bruno of the *Washington Post* wrote, "In April 2008, Petraeus echoed those gains in testimony before U.S. lawmakers. Tips from Sunni volunteers have 'reduced significantly' al-Qaeda in Iraq's ability to strike, the general said, and have increased the number of weapons caches uncovered and confiscated."

In view of the volume of analysis provided by past and contemporary counterinsurgency scholars, and in light of recent and ongoing counterinsurgency operations, this thesis explores the key considerations for irregular security forces in counterinsurgency. Using the theme discussed above, this thesis examines two conflicts and presents case studies of the campaigns in Dhofar, Oman, from 1965 to 1975 and in Iraq during Operation IRAQI FREEDOM. This body of work will attempt to demonstrate the value of irregular security forces while also dispelling any ideas that such forces in themselves constitute a silver bullet or an associated counter to insurgent threats.

Notes

1.   Frank Kitson, *Low Intensity Operations* (London: Faber and Faber, 1972), 15. "The important point to notice is that guerrilla warfare is described as a traditional form of conflict, and that it has been used throughout history either independently or in conjunction with orthodox operations. In fact, comments on the conduct of such operations were included in a book written as long ago as the fourth century B.C. by the Chinese general Sun Tzu, which still makes sense and which Mao Tse Tung is known to have studied when formulating his own ideas on the subject."

2.   Daniel Marston and Carter Malkasian, eds., *Counterinsurgency in Modern Warfare* (Oxford: Osprey Publishing, 2010), 13. "After being neglected in the aftermath of the Vietnam War, the study of counterinsurgency returned to prominence in the early years of the 21st century as a result of the wars in Iraq and Afghanistan."

3.   Jonathan M. House, *Combined Arms Warfare in the Twentieth Century* (Lawrence, KS: University Press of Kansas, 2001), 190. "Moreover, nuclear deterrence made it seem suicidal for two nuclear powers to fight directly; instead, the United States and the Soviet Union fought a series of proxy conflicts, in which one or both sides provided aid to lesser allies while maintaining the fiction that the two superpowers were at peace with each other."

4. Department of the Army, Field Manual 3-24, *Counterinsurgency* (Washington, DC: Government Printing Office, 2006), vii. "Counterinsurgency operations generally have been neglected in broader American military doctrine and national security policies since the end of the Vietnam War over 30 years ago."

5.   House, *Combined Arms Warfare in the Twentieth Century,* 239. "The West German government's desire to protect every kilometer of its shallow territory obligated the U.S. Army to defend along the interzonal border established in 1945, with little opportunity for delaying or maneuver tactics. At least during the first battles of such a war, the U.S. Army would have to fight outnumbered and outgunned by a superior Soviet foe."

6.   House, *Combined Arms Warfare in the Twentieth Century,* 240. "The How-to-Fight manuals described offensive operations as well as maneuver when on the defensive, but they seemed to emphasize a desperate struggle against overwhelming odds, much like that fought by Israeli tankers on the Golan Heights at the start of the 1973 war. Using the ROAD divisional structure, cross-attached task forces and teams of infantry and armor would fight from hull-down positions. Minefields would slow down the enemy advance, after which antitank guided missiles at long range and faster firing tank guns at short range would whittle down a huge attacking force. The defenders would rely on firepower more than on maneuver or initiative."

7.   House, *Combined Arms Warfare in the Twentieth Century,* 246. "For centuries, tactics had been based on firing a huge volume of shells at the enemy, even though only a small percentage ever found their targets. In the late twentieth century, however, the advent of guided bombs, cruise missiles, and individually fired missiles changed this equation fundamentally, making a few, relatively

inexpensive, weapons far more effective than thousands of dumb bombs and shells."

8.   Training and Doctrine Command, TRADOC PAM 525-3-0, *The Army Capstone Concept: Operational Adaptability—Operating Under Conditions of Uncertainty and Complexity in an Era of Persistent Conflict* (Fort Monroe, VA: Government Printing Office, 2009), 6. "In the 1990s, many argued that United States' (U.S.) competitive advantages in communications, information, and precision strike technologies had brought about a revolution in military affairs (RMA). RMA advocates, however, neglected many of the continuities of armed conflict and did not recognize the limitations of new technologies and emerging military capabilities. In particular, concepts that relied mainly on the ability to target enemy forces with long range precision munitions separated war from its political, cultural, and psychological contexts. Some of this work focused on how U.S. forces might prefer to fight and then assumed that preference was relevant to the problem of future war. Literature describing the RMA and the movement known as defense transformation was rooted in the belief that surveillance, communications, and information technologies would dramatically improve battlespace knowledge, eliminate surprise, and permit U.S. forces to achieve full spectrum dominance through the employment of precision-strike capabilities. Concepts and ideas with labels such as network-centric warfare, rapid decisive operations, and shock and awe, entailed the application of leap-ahead capabilities that would enable small networked forces to win wars quickly and at low cost. RMA and defense transformation-related thinking influenced Army doctrine, organization, and modernization."

9.   Lieutenant Colonel Herbert R. McMaster, "Crack in the Foundation: Defense Transformation and the Underlying Assumption of Dominant Knowledge in Future War" (Research Projects, U.S. Army War College, Carlisle Barracks, Pennsylvania, 2003), 9.

10.   For a rich debate on this topic, visit the *Small Wars Journal* "On War Modifiers" debate posted 6 March 2009, http://smallwarsjournal.com/blog/2009/03/print/on-war-modifiers/ (accessed 27 April 2011).

11.   General George W. Casey Jr., "The Army of the 21st Century," *ARMY* (October 2009): 28.

12.   Marston and Malkasian, *Counterinsurgency in Modern Warfare*, 15. "General Sir Frank Kitson (British Army) wrote *Low Intensity Operations* in 1971. Kitson served in the anti-Mau-Mau, Malayan Emergency, Oman, Cyprus, and Northern Ireland operations."

13.   Kitson, *Low Intensity Operations,* 2. "In writing on this subject one of the most difficult problems concerns the matter of terminology. The British Army gives separate definitions of Civil Disturbance, Insurgency, Guerilla Warfare, Subversion, Terrorism, Civil Disobedience, Communist Revolutionary Warfare, and Insurrection on the one hand and of Counter Insurgency, Internal Security, and Counter Revolutionary Operations on the other. Elsewhere conflicts are variously described as Partisan, Irregular or Unconventional Wars, and the people taking part in them have an even wider selection of labels attached to them. Furthermore, although a particular author will use one of these terms to cover one aspect of the business and another to cover another, a different author will use the same two

terms in a totally different way."

14. FM 3-24, Glossary-4.

15. Ministry of Defence, British Army Field Manual Volume 1 Part 10, *Countering Insurgency* (London: Ministry of Defense, 2010), 1-4.

16. FM 3-24, Glossary-5.

17. British Army Field Manual Volume 1 Part 10, 1-4.

18. John Mackinlay, *The Insurgent Archipelago*, (London:C. Hurst and Co. Ltd., 2009), 70-71.

19. David Kilcullen, *Counterinsurgency*, (New York:Oxford University Press, 2010), 1. On page 2, Kilcullen further defines counterinsurgency, "Indeed, if you cut the qualifying adjectives out of the field manual's [FM 3-24] definition of counterinsurgency, you are left only with 'actions taken by a government to defeat insurgency.' This truncated definition shows that there is no template, no single set of techniques, for countering insurgencies. Counterinsurgency is, simply, whatever governments do to defeat rebellions. Thus, the character of any particular conflict is impossible to understand without reference to three defining factors: the nature of the insurgency being countered, the nature of the government being supported, and the environment – especially the human environment – in which the conflict takes place."

20. Marston and Malkasian, *Counterinsurgency in Modern Warfare,*, 13. "There are three 'key' theorists from this period, whose works are still influential: Colonel David Galula, *Counterinsurgency Warfare Theory and Practice*, Sir Robert Thompson, and General Sir Frank Kitson."

21. Kitson, *Low Intensity Operations*, 3.

22. Marston and Malkasian, *Counterinsurgency in Modern Warfare,*, 14. "Sir Robert Thompson wrote *Defeating Communist Insurgency* in 1966, outlining the lessons of his experiences in the Malayan Emergency."

23. Sir Robert Thompson, *Defeating Communist Insurgency: The Lessons of Malaya and Vietnam*, (New York: Frederick Praeger, 1967), 28.

24. Marston and Malkasian, *Counterinsurgency in Modern Warfare*, 13. "Colonel David Galula was a French officer who served from 1965-58 in the Algerian War of Independence. His book, *Counterinsurgency Warfare: Theory and Practice*, was written in 1964, based upon his experiences in Algeria."

25. David Galula, *Counterinsurgency Warfare Theory and Practice*, (Florida: Hailer, 2005), 44-58. Galula describes the orthodox or communist pattern for revolutionary warfare as a five-step process. The first step is the creation of a political party. The second step is to build up support for the party. In the third step, guerrilla warfare, armed struggle continues the political struggle when political action and subversion have failed to allow the insurgents to seize power. Movement warfare is the fourth step. It is required to defeat the counterinsurgents' conventional forces. In the final step, the annihilation campaign, the insurgents conduct offensive operations to complete the destruction of the counterinsurgents.

26. Galula, *Counterinsurgency Warfare Theory and Practice*, 4.

27. Galula, *Counterinsurgency Warfare Theory and Practice*, 63. "From the

counterinsurgent's point of view, a revolutionary war can be divided into two periods: 1. The 'cold revolutionary war,' when the insurgent's activity remains on the whole legal and nonviolent … 2. The 'hot revolutionary war,' when the insurgent's activity becomes openly illegal and violent …"

28. Roger Trinquier, *Modern Warfare: A French View of Counterinsurgency*, (New York: Frederick Praeger, 1964), 8-9. "In *modern warfare*, we are not actually grappling with an army organized along traditional lines, but with a few armed elements acting clandestinely within a population manipulated by a special organization. … In seeking a solution, it is essential to realize that in *modern warfare* we are not up against just a few armed bands spread across a given territory, but rather against an *armed clandestine organization* whose essential role is to impose its will upon the population. Victory will be obtained only through the complete destruction of that organization. This is the master concept that must guide us in our study of *modern warfare*."

29. Trinquier, *Modern Warfare*, 6.

30. Carl von Clausewitz, *On War*, ed. and trans. Michael Howard and Peter Paret (Princeton, NJ: Princeton University Press, 1976), 88–9.

31. H.R. McMaster, "On War: Lessons to be Learned," in *Survival: Global Politics and Strategy*, 50, no. 1 (2008): 27.

32. FM 3-24, 6-22.

33. For a detailed description of the Dhofar campaign, refer to the Dhofar case study in this paper.

34. Robert Komer, *The Malayan Emergency in Retrospect: Organization of a Successful Counterinsurgency Effort*. (Santa Monica: RAND, 1972), 38-41.

35. For a detailed description of the Malayan Emergency and the elements of the successful strategy, see Daniel Marston, "The Indian Army, Partition, and the Punjab Boundary Force, 1945-1947," *War in History* 16, no. 4 (2009): 469-505; Richard Stubbs, "From Search and Destroy to Hearts and Minds: The Evolution of British Strategy in Malaya 1948-60," in *Counterinsurgency in Modern Warfare,* eds. Daniel Marston and Carter Malkasian (Oxford: Osprey Publishing, 2010), 101-118; Robert Komer, *The Malayan Emergency in Retrospect: Organization of a Successful Counterinsurgency Effort* (Santa Monica: RAND, 1972), http:// www.rand.org/pubs/reports/R957/ (accessed 23 April 2011), 25-68; John Coates, *Suppressing Insurgency* (Boulder, CO: Westview Press, 1992), 77-108; James Corum, *Training Indigenous Forces in Counterinsurgency: A Tale of Two Insurgencies,* http://www.strategicstudiesinstitute.army.mil/ pubs/display. cfm?PubID=648 (accessed 23 April 2011), 1-24, 34-54.

36. FM 3-24 discusses the principles and paradoxes of counterinsurgency on pages 1-20 thru 1-28, and in AFM 1:10 (2010) on pages 3-1 thru 3-16.

37. McMaster, *Crack in the Foundation,* 61. "Enthusiasm for impressive new technologies connected by the network into a 'system of systems' led many to conclude prior to Operation Iraqi Freedom that those capabilities represented a 'silver bullet' solution to the complex problem of war."

38. Marston and Malkasian, *Counterinsurgency in Modern Warfare*, 13-14.

39. Galula, *Counterinsurgency Warfare Theory and Practice*, 87.

40. Galula, *Counterinsurgency Warfare Theory and Practice*, 89.

41. Galula, *Counterinsurgency Warfare Theory and Practice*, 87. "The expected result — final defeat of the insurgents — is not an addition but a multiplication of these various operations; they are all essential and if one is nil, the product will be zero."

42. Galula, *Counterinsurgency Warfare Theory and Practice*, 75. "The population, therefore, becomes the objective for the counterinsurgent as it was for his enemy. Its tacit support, its submission to law and order, its consensus — taken for granted in normal times — have been undermined by the insurgent's activity. And the truth is that the insurgent, with his organization at the grass roots, is tactically the strongest of opponents where it counts, at the population level. This is where the fight has to be conducted, in spite of the counterinsurgent's ideological handicap and in spite of the head start gained by the insurgent in organizing the population."

43. Galula, *Counterinsurgency Warfare Theory and Practice*, 75-76.

44. Galula, *Counterinsurgency Warfare Theory and Practice*, 78-79.

45. Galula, *Counterinsurgency Warfare Theory and Practice*, 79. Galula's fourth law is "Intensity of efforts and vastness of means are essential."

46. Thompson, *Defeating Communist Insurgency*, 50-58. Thompson's principles are: "*First principle.* The government must have a clear political aim: to establish and maintain a free, independent and united country which is politically and economically stable and viable. ...*Second principle.* The government must function in accordance with law. ... *Third principle.* The government must have an overall plan. ... *Fourth principle.* The government must give priority to defeating the political subversion, not the guerillas. ...*Fifth principle.* In the guerilla phase of an insurgency, a government must secure its base areas first."

47. Thompson, *Defeating Communist Insurgency*, 111. "As already stated in the basic principles, the government must have an overall plan to co-ordinate all military and civil effort and to lay down priorities. The plan must also take into account the fourth and fifth principles that the main emphasis should be given to defeating subversion, not the guerillas, and that the government must secure its base areas first. When applying this to action and operations on the ground, there will be four definite stages which can be summed up as clearing, holding, winning, and won."

48. Thompson, *Defeating Communist Insurgency*, 111-112.

49. FM 3-24, 5-22 thru 5-23.

50. This is based on the author's personal experience as the plans officer for the 3d ACR during the pre-deployment training period which included seminar discussions between the Regimental Commander and his subordinate commanders, as well as a reading list which included several of the counterinsurgency classics.

51. Chief of the General Staff in the UK at the time of publication

52. Kitson, *Low Intensity Operations*, xi. Included in the foreword by General Carver.

53. Marston and Malkasian, *Counterinsurgency in Modern Warfare*, 15.

54. Kitson, *Low Intensity Operations*, 96. "A cow can turn grass into milk but a further process is required in order to turn the milk into butter. Two separate functions are therefore involved in putting troops into contact with insurgents. The first one consists of collecting background information, and the second involves developing it into contact information."

55. Kitson, *Low Intensity Operations*, 96. "Two separate functions are therefore involved in putting troops into contact with insurgents."

56. Kitson, *Low Intensity Operations*, 96.

57. Kitson, *Low Intensity Operations*, 98-99. "Clearly, if a commander is going to operate in this way it means that he must be prepared to devote an immense amount of his time, thought, and energy to handling information."

58. Kitson, *Low Intensity Operations*, 99.

59. Kitson, *Low Intensity Operations*, 200.

60. Kilcullen, *Counterinsurgency*, 26-27.

61. Kilcullen, *Counterinsurgency*, 26. "Twenty-Eight Articles" has been published numerous times in periodicals such as *Military Review,* the *Marine Corps Gazette,* and FM 3-24.

62. A newly annotated version of "Twenty-Eight Articles" is included in David Kilcullen, *Counterinsurgency*, (New York: Oxford University Press, 2010), 30-49.

63. Marston and Malkasian, *Counterinsurgency in Modern Warfare*, 18.

64. Marston and Malkasian, *Counterinsurgency in Modern Warfare*, 18.

65. Marston and Malkasian, *Counterinsurgency in Modern Warfare*, 18.

66. Marston and Malkasian, *Counterinsurgency in Modern Warfare*, 19. "This book does not endorse any single explanation for success in counterinsurgency. As this list shows, the whole process of waging a successful counterinsurgency campaign is delicate and complex, requiring nuanced understanding and flexibility on the part of all involved."

67. General Stanley A. McChrystal, U.S. Army, Commander, US Forces-Afghanistan, Commander, International Security Assistance Force-Afghanistan, "Eight Imperatives for Success in Afghanistan From 'Commander's Initial Guidance,' 13 June 2009," *Military Review*, (July-August 2009): 136. "1. Protect and Partner with the People. We are fighting for the Afghan people—not against them. Our focus on their welfare will build the trust and support necessary for success. 2. Conduct a Comprehensive Counterinsurgency Campaign. Insurgencies fail when root causes disappear. Security is essential, but I believe our ultimate success lies in partnering with the Afghan Government, partner nations, NGOs, and others to build the foundations of good government and economic development. 3. Understand the Environment. We must understand in detail the situation, however complex, and be able to explain it to others. Our ability to act effectively demands a real appreciation for the positive and negative impact of everything we do — or fail to do. Understanding is a prerequisite for success. 4. Ensure Values Underpin our Effort. We must demonstrate through our words and actions our commitment to fair play, our respect and sensitivity for the cultures and traditions of others, and

an understanding that rules of law and humanity do not end when fighting starts. Both our goals and conduct must be admired. 5. Listen Closely-Speak Clearly. We must listen to understand—and speak clearly to be understood. Communicating our intentions and accurately reflecting our actions to all audiences is a critical responsibility—and necessity. 6. Act as One Team. We are an alliance of nations with different histories, cultures, and national objectives united in our support for Afghanistan. We must be unified in purpose, forthright in communication, and committed to each other. 7. Constantly Adapt. This war is unique, and our ability to respond to even subtle changes in conditions will be decisive. I ask you to challenge conventional wisdom and abandon practices that are ingrained into many military cultures. And I ask you to push me to do the same. 8. Act with Courage and Resolve. Hard fighting, difficult decisions, and inevitable losses will mark the days ahead. Each of us, from our most junior personnel to our senior leaders, must display physical, mental, and moral courage. Our partners must trust our commitment; enemies must not question our resolve."

68. General Martin E. Dempsey, "The Army Capstone Concept and Institutional Adaptation," *Landpower Essay* 10-1 (March 2010): 3, http://www.ausa.org/ publications/ilw/Documents/LPE10-1.pdf (accessed 31 May 2011).

69. Trinquier, *Modern Warfare*, 92.

70. Training and Doctrine Command, TRADOC PAM 525-3-0, 28.

71. Najim Abed Al-Jabouri and Sterling Jensen, "The Iraqi and AQI Roles in the Sunni Awakening," *PRISM* 2, no. 1 (2010): 11. "The people were hoping for someone to take a stand against AQI. Abdul Sattar started stating openly what people were thinking (but did not dare to say publicly): that al Qaeda and Iran were the real occupiers in Iraq, not the Americans. Then, on September 9, 2006, Abdul Sattar and Faisal Gaoud — a former governor of Anbar and representative of the tribal elite residing in Amman who had been soliciting U.S. support for an Awakening since 2004 — announced the Anbar Awakening. In his guestroom, in the presence of the 1–1 AD commander as well as over a dozen of his tribal peers, Abdul Sattar boldly declared that the American troops were "friendly forces" and "guests in Anbar." This topic is discussed in detail in the Iraq case study.

72. Najim and Jensen, "The Iraqi and AQI Roles in the Sunni Awakening," 14. "In an effort to expand the influence of the Awakening, General Petraeus started the Sons of Iraq program for operations in Diyala and Baghdad, usually paying Sunni tribesmen in al Qaeda-infested areas to work as paramilitaries with the hope that someday they would be integrated into the Ministry of the Interior."

73. Najim and Jensen, "The Iraqi and AQI Roles in the Sunni Awakening," 12. "As Sheikh Sattar was successful in gaining U.S. support in police recruitment, his popularity and influence grew."

74. Najim and Jensen, "The Iraqi and AQI Roles in the Sunni Awakening," 11.

75. Colonel Wayne Grigsby, DefenseLink News Transcript: DOD News Briefing with Colonel Grigsby from Iraq, https://digitalndulibrary.ndu.edu/cdm4/document.php? CISOROOT=/merln&CISOPTR=7324&REC=1, (accessed on 13 May 2011). As an example, Sons of Iraq are noted in this quote as assisting in holding and controlling areas cleared of insurgents. "For instance, where al

Qaeda and other Sunni extremist groups had their run in the southern portion of our battlespace, now we estimate there are three Sunni extremist groups of no more than 10 personnel per group in our battlespace, disrupted and not able to synchronize operations. We killed or captured their leaders, denied them use of safe houses and support zones and with our Sons of Iraq allies we are sitting in the former resupply lines, holding the terrain, not letting the extremists come back in."

76. Captain Pete Hegseth, "Sons of Iraq: A grassroots surge against al-Qaeda," *National Review Online*, http://www.nationalreview.com/articles/223811/sons-iraq/pete-hegseth (accessed 13 May 2011). "The importance of these forces can hardly be overstated. After American and national Iraqi forces clear an area of insurgents, the Sons of Iraq remain to *hold* the neighborhood and protect the population, driving out the final remnants of resistance."

77. James Corum, *Training Indigenous Forces in Counterinsurgency: A Tale of Two Insurgencies*. http://www.strategicstudiesinstitute.army.mil/pubs/ display. cfm?PubID=648, (accessed 13 March 2011): 36.

78. Hegseth, "Sons of Iraq," 3. "The Sons are not nearly as well trained as their Iraqi army and police counterparts, but to a man, they *expect* to eventually become formally recognized as trained Iraqi police. They want to serve their country in uniform and — as soon as conditions permit — without consideration of sectarian background."

79. Hegseth, "Sons of Iraq," 2. "All Sons of Iraq and their leadership are required to be residents of the neighborhoods they protect and are not allowed to enforce law outside their assigned area or to conduct offensive operations."

Chapter 2
Raising Irregular Security Forces

> A victory is not the destruction in a given area of the insurgent's forces and his political organization. ... A victory is that plus the permanent isolation of the insurgent from the population, isolation not enforced upon the population but maintained by and with the population.

> David Galula, *Counterinsurgency Warfare*

This paper explores the key considerations for irregular security forces in counterinsurgency. These factors include purpose, strategy, threat, composition, legitimacy, training, location of employment, leadership, partnership, advisory, and scope. The remainder of this chapter defines irregular security forces and discusses the factors listed above.

US Army doctrine defines irregular forces as "Armed individuals or groups who are not members of the regular armed forces, police, or other internal security forces."[1] For the purpose of this paper, the term irregular security forces refers to indigenous security forces, not part of the regular police or military organizations of the host nation. Irregular security forces recruit from the local population to provide a basic level of security in a given area. Examples of irregular security forces include the Philippine Constabulary,[2] the *Firqat* in Dhofar,[3] and the Sons of Iraq.[4] Other common terms for irregular security forces include militias, auxiliaries, and paramilitary forces.

Irregular security forces generally do not clear areas of insurgents, but rather conduct security operations to hold an area after regular forces (e.g. army,[5] police) have cleared it in order to prevent the insurgents from regaining control.[6] Irregular security forces operate where they live to secure their own clansmen, tribesmen, families, or communities. Irregular security forces generally do not conduct operations outside of the local area from which the host nation or intervening power recruits them.

Because irregular security forces usually operate where they live, they are the first line of defense against insurgent attempts to infiltrate, re-infiltrate, intimidate, or recruit members of the population to support the insurgency. Although army forces can provide this first line of defense, they are not the force best suited to the task. Army forces train to locate, close with, and destroy enemy forces. Army approaches often involve ample use of firepower and may result in collateral damage. For example, Major General C. H. Boucher, General Officer Commanding at the outset of the Malayan Emergency, initially saw the campaign as a conventional war, and subsequently directed soldiers to respond to violence with greater violence, shoot to kill, and conduct large-scale sweeps to locate and destroy enemy persons, factions, and supporters.[7]

Because they are a national force versus a local force, army forces often operate outside their home areas and therefore lack any connection to the local population.[8] When army forces operate in a particular area, it is usually for a short-term operation which, when contrasted to irregular security forces that operate in the area permanently, creates a more limited level of situational understanding. Additionally, employing army forces in local security duties consumes offensive capabilities possibly needed elsewhere.[9] Because army forces take longer to train and equip than irregular security forces, a host nation may give development of army forces a lower priority when battling an insurgency. This is especially likely when the host nation faces no external conventional threats, or when a capable interventionist power is present to assist the host nation and deter external aggression.

Police forces[10] are generally better suited to local security than are army forces.[11] Police seek to prevent violence if possible and, because they generally live in the area where they operate, are in constant contact with the local populace. As with army forces, police also require extensive training, equipment, and infrastructure (e.g. headquarters or precinct buildings, vehicles, communications equipment), and therefore require more time and resources to form. When counterinsurgents form improperly trained police forces, these forces often tend to exacerbate the situation through heavy-handed tactics and corruption.[12]

When drawn from the population, irregular security forces have several inherent advantages (e.g. knowledge of local terrain, normal patterns of life and social structure, and shared interests in the welfare of the community) over other types of security forces, which combine to make them effective sources of intelligence.[13] In contrast to army or police units, counterinsurgents can raise irregular forces relatively quickly. These rapidly raised irregular security forces can be effective without extensive training or a large amount of materiel support. This reduces the amount of resources that counterinsurgents must divert from regular security forces, and allows the regular security forces to focus on offensive operations versus static security duties.[14] Because of the unique capabilities and characteristics of irregular security forces, the host nation may choose to raise them even if it has the capability and capacity to raise regular forces.

It is important to note at this point that while irregular security forces can potentially fill a security gap more quickly than regular forces can, this is only a short-term solution. Defeating insurgencies often requires a long-term approach involving development or expansion of regular forces.[15] The development of regular security forces may involve the incorporation of some of the irregular forces into the regular security forces or the formalization of the irregular forces as was the case in the Philippines[16] and Malaya[17] respectively. The government of Iraq initially overlooked the benefits of transitioning irregular security forces to regular security forces after the formation of the Sons of Iraq, many of whom sought inclusion into a more long-term security force.[18]

Purpose

In order to develop appropriate irregular security forces, host nations and/or intervening powers must understand and clearly articulate the security requirements that irregular security forces will address. For example, if the purpose of irregular security forces is to deny insurgent access to the population by conducting patrols around a secured population center at night, as was the case with the Home Guard in the Malayan Emergency,[19] then the level of training required for irregular security forces may be low. Other potential purposes for irregular forces may include assisting in population control,[20] intelligence gathering, fixed site security,[21] performing surveillance of local areas, or augmenting regular forces during limited offensive operations. Without a clear purpose for irregular security forces, the host nation or intervening power cannot apply the appropriate resources to train, equip, and employ those forces.

To develop a clear purpose for irregular security forces, the host nation must first understand several aspects of the campaign such as the enemy situation, and the availability of regular forces to support and advise irregular forces on a daily basis.[22] Other aspects include the drivers of conflict fueling the insurgency, the sentiments of the population in the area of employment, the composition of the society among which the irregular forces will operate, and the capacity of the host nation to train, equip, and control the irregular force. Each localized area within a counterinsurgency campaign has unique conditions – what works in one situation may not work in another. Understanding these key aspects will enable the host nation to raise the right kind of force for each unique set of conditions in each local area of employment.

Strategy

The overall strategy of the counterinsurgency campaign, which shifts as the campaign unfolds, weighs heavily in making the determination between quality and quantity. In the Malayan Emergency, the initial response to the insurgency was to recruit large numbers (quantity) of security forces (to include both regular and irregular forces).[23] In the case of the Home Guards in Malaya, the government action to raise a massive number of irregular security forces provided temporary stability, but did not stop the insurgency from swelling its ranks.[24] A similar effort to expand rapidly host nation security forces is currently underway in Afghanistan.[25]

As the counterinsurgency campaign in Malaya progressed, the need to reform and retrain the rapidly raised and poorly trained security forces became apparent. The quality of security forces became more important than quantity.[26] As James Corum stated in *Training Indigenous Forces in*

Counterinsurgency: A Tale of Two Insurgencies, regarding police forces in Malaya,

> It is better to suffer from a shortage of officers than to have sufficient numbers, but many of those incompetent or corrupt. A corrupt police and military culture is of enormous benefit to the insurgents. ... In the long run, it is cheaper to spend the money up front to build effective police and security forces than to spend less and end up with corrupt and abusive forces that alienate the population.[27]

The development of irregular security forces must be flexible and adaptable to changes in the campaign. The host nation must recognize that the type of forces required in the early stages of the campaign may not be the same as those needed later. The host nation institutions that generate security forces require both short-term and long-term capacities to meet early requirements while still building toward end-state security capability goals.

In the French counterinsurgency campaign in Algeria from 1954 to 1962 for example, the contemporary strategy, known as *quadrillage,* meaning framework or grid, was to employ static forces to secure populated areas as well as mobile reserves that could conduct operations between the secured populated areas as well as reinforce the static forces as required.[28] In order to employ this strategy, the French forces would require 120,000 irregular forces recruited from the population to augment security operations. To gain sufficient popular support to enable recruitment of such a large number of forces would require the French first to secure the populated areas.[29] As David Galula observed in *Counterinsurgency Warfare: Theory and Practice,* "If the counterinsurgent is so strong as to be able to saturate the entire country with garrisons, military operations along conventional lines will, of course work. The insurgent, unable to grow beyond a certain level, will slowly wither away. But saturation can seldom be afforded."[30]

In contrast to the French strategy in Algeria, a recommended approach devised in Vietnam known as the oil-blot or oil-spot approach was to establish security in one local area and then extend the control of security forces outward gradually.[31] Once regular security forces clear an area, and the host nation establishes irregular security forces to hold the area, regular security forces can then continue offensive operations to clear additional areas. Where *quadrillage* envisions gaining influence over all of the critical areas simultaneously,[32] the oil-blot or oil-spot approach seeks a slow expansion of control, or in modern parlance, clear-hold-build. In these two brief examples, the impact of strategy on the scope of irregular security force development becomes readily apparent, as a *quadrillage-*like approach requires a large amount of forces throughout where an oil-spot approach requires a steady increase in forces over time.

24

Threat

Irregular security forces must be able to survive encounters with the insurgents in their area of operations. This requires some level of training, equipping, and force protection.[33] Based on the local conditions, irregular security forces may require different types of equipment to include small arms, heavy weapons, communications equipment, and vehicles. Irregular security forces may be easier to intimidate or drive away if the insurgents have significantly greater firepower.

In rural areas, irregular security forces may require vehicles in order to patrol large open areas or to post and support personnel at checkpoints. In urban areas where vehicular traffic is high, irregular security forces may require greater force protection measures to counter car bombs and suicide attacks. The use of small arms by irregular security forces requires training to instill confidence and proficiency. As additional types of equipment become necessary based on local conditions, the training requirements increase.

When irregular security forces make contact with enemy forces, they may also require the means to request and receive responsive support from regular forces depending upon the capabilities of the insurgents.[34] As discussed later, partnership between regular and irregular security force units or embedding trained advisers with irregular forces may better enable irregular forces to access capabilities normally found only in regular forces (e.g. aviation support, fire support).

Composition

Forces drawn from the local population best secure cleared areas.[35] Drawing forces from local areas not only ties the local population to the government, but also increases the effectiveness of the irregular force in intelligence gathering[36] as they are familiar with the local area and population. Additionally, when the host nation recruits irregular forces representative of the local population (e.g. ethnic, tribal, religious), it creates opportunities for disaffected segments of the population.[37]

Failing to develop forces representative of the population can result in greater resistance to government control. As a case in point, the Catholic minority in Northern Ireland saw itself as the target of security forces predominately of Protestant composition and sympathy.[38] The highly sectarian Iraqi Security Forces provides another example. As Najim Abed al Jabouri, the former mayor of Tal Afar noted, Sunnis seeking assistance in raising irregular security forces "were generally from the mixed cities in Salah al-Din, Diyala, and Baghdad, where the Iraqi Police were already well established but were heavily sectarian. … In these heterogeneous areas, the Iraqi Police were often an instrument for sectarian violence where Sunnis sought a means to defend themselves legally."[39]

Legitimacy

Irregular security forces are important not only for the added security capability they provide to the counterinsurgent's forces, but also because they demonstrate a connection of the will of the people to the government[40] and away from the insurgents.[41] This does not imply that the formation of irregular security forces equates to wholehearted support of the entire population for the government. It does signal that the population has taken a step away from the insurgents and toward the government. David Galula's principle of irreversibility applies here:

> When troops live among the population and give it protection until the population is able to protect itself with a minimum of outside support, the insurgent's power cannot easily be rebuilt, and this in itself is no mean achievement. But the turning point really comes when leaders have emerged from the population and have committed themselves on the side of the counterinsurgent. They can be counted upon because they have proved their loyalty in deeds and not in words, and because they have everything to lose from a return of the insurgents.[42]

Local populations must see irregular security forces as legitimate and representative of the social and ethnic groups that comprise those populations. This requires consultation with local leaders, ethnic and racial representation, and possibly some level of control over the local security forces wielded by the community. Failure to create security forces representative of the local community will likely alienate segments of the population, which may encourage their support to the insurgency. As seen in Malaya, recruiting from disaffected groups of the population can result in broader support for the government, thus limiting the undecided pool of potential recruits for the insurgency.[43] As stated in a 2007 study by RAND, "The use of indigenous forces, especially forces from the particular area in question, increases the legitimacy of the counterinsurgents and can also help to divide and weaken the insurgency by psychologically unhinging the insurgents."[44] Support of the local population is also critical to irregular security forces as they serve as a source of information on insurgent activity in the local area[45] and can provide irregular forces with early warning of an impending attack or the emplacement of an improvised explosive device or ambush.[46]

By allowing a local population to raise irregular security forces, the host nation government provides an outlet for the natural desire of the people to respond to the threat posed by insurgents by providing for the defense of their own interests (e.g. family, business, tribe, ethnic group).[47] Another aspect of legitimacy is the desire or willingness of the local population to support the host nation government and join the security forces.[48] Sources of such desire to participate vary based on the nature of the conflict, the grievances of the population, the local perceptions of the government and the insurgent organization, and the likelihood of one side or the other to prevail in the conflict. Sir Robert Thompson described the natural desire to end up on the victorious side: "What the peasant wants to know is does the government mean to win the war because if not, he will have to support the insurgent."[49]

In Dhofar for example, the tribesmen of the *Jebel* fought on both the insurgent and host nation sides in varying degrees over the course of the campaign. Once Qaboos, the son of the Sultan of Oman, overthrew his father and assumed the throne, he enacted sweeping reforms that addressed many of the grievances fueling support for the insurgency to include amnesty for those willing to join the Sultan's forces against the insurgents. As the new Sultan addressed the grievances and began to show greater aptitude and resolve to defeat the insurgency, many of the *Jebeli* tribesmen quit the insurgency and joined with the Sultan.[50]

Among the reforms enacted by Sultan Qaboos after deposing his father were lifting of sanctions against education, technology (e.g. modern medicine, movies, radios), and movement within Oman and to other countries. One of the key reforms that contributed to increased popular support for the Sultan was recruitment of irregular forces from within Dhofar, especially from among the tribes living on the *jebel*. The recruitment effort was initially indirect and involved dispatching Civil Aid Teams[51] that included medical personnel to provide care for the local populace in Taqa and Mirbat. Initially, only women and children came forth to receive treatment for chronic ailments. As word of effective treatment spread, men from the local tribes began to appear seeking treatment, which created opportunities for the Sultan's representatives to engage and recruit for the *firqats*.[52]

As the inclusion of Dhofaris in the Sultan's Armed Forces in the form of tribally-based *firqats* expanded, the local perceptions of these forces improved. No longer did Dhofaris view the Sultan's forces as an army of occupation once they had opportunity to join.[53] Although the *firqats* were irregular forces with dubious utility in the eyes of traditional military observers, the Sultan paid and supplied them like any other military force, which increased their legitimacy in the eyes of the population.[54]

Despite outward appearances and the difficulties of employing *firqats*, they were invaluable to the Sultan's Armed Forces for their abilities in "reconnaissance, gathering intelligence and communicating with the nomadic population."[55]

Indeed, Ian Gardiner, who operated with various *firqats* in the Dhofar campaign, stated the following regarding the value of these irregular forces: "For all their limitations, I do not believe we could have won the war without the *Firqat*."[56]

Location of Employment

In addition to the purpose and scope, it is important to determine where irregular security forces will operate as part of the plan to develop them. While the counterinsurgency strategy may require irregular security forces in several locations throughout the area of operations, the host nation must establish priorities for these locations based on the enemy situation and the host nation's ability, and potential interventionist ability, to provide support in order to raise irregular security forces appropriate to the situation. David Galula's Fourth Law in counterinsurgency operations dictates that the counterinsurgent cannot dilute his forces and hope to gain sustainable progress, but must "[concentrate] efforts, resources, and personnel" in order to secure the population and gain support by providing the population with confidence that the counterinsurgent side will prevail.[57]

With Galula's Fourth Law in mind, the host nation must determine where initial success is most likely. If the counterinsurgent force has sufficient strength, it may focus initially on the most difficult areas where the insurgents enjoy strong support and freedom to operate, and then move on to areas less contested. If the counterinsurgent force is relatively weak, the host nation may choose to consolidate the areas it controls and move gradually toward the more difficult areas.[58] When determining the relative strength of the opposing sides, the host nation must look beyond the military aspects (e.g. number of troops, types of equipment, mobility), and factor in the political and social dimensions (e.g. whether the population in a particular area more likely to sympathize with the government or the insurgency).[59] Determining the most viable approach should factor into the size, quality, and location of employment of irregular and regular forces.

The host nation must also consider the willingness of the population to join and support irregular forces. This willingness is often dependent upon where the forces will conduct operations. Popular support and willingness on the part of the population to join irregular security forces increase when irregular forces operate in their local area. In Vietnam, for example, drafted recruits were often required to operate far from their home areas, which went against the cultural norms of the rural population and caused many potential draftees to seek refuge among the insurgent camps to avoid service.[60] Aside from cultural considerations such as those in Vietnam, local communities want their efforts, their blood and treasure, to go toward providing security locally.

Training

As Dr. Daniel Marston wrote, "Proper training and build-up of local indigenous forces is key to clearing and holding any contested region in a successful counterinsurgency campaign."[61] Irregular security force training requirements vary based on the local conditions of the area in which they will operate. To determine the appropriate skills and corresponding training requirements of irregular security forces, counterinsurgents must understand the other factors mentioned at the beginning of this chapter – purpose, strategy, threat, composition, legitimacy, location of employment, leadership, partnership, advisory, and scope. As FM 3-24 advises, counterinsurgents must employ irregular security forces in limited roles initially to build confidence and avoid politically costly defeat:

> Committing poorly trained and badly led forces results in high casualties and invites tactical defeats. While defeat in a small operation may have little strategic consequence in a conventional war, even a small tactical defeat of HN forces can have serious strategic consequences in a COIN. Insurgent warfare is largely about perceptions. Effective insurgent leaders can quickly turn minor wins into major propaganda victories. Defeat of one government force can quickly degrade the morale of others. If a HN force fails, the local populace may begin to lose confidence in the government's ability to protect them.[62]

Regardless of the exact capabilities that irregular security forces require, counterinsurgents must enforce some key elements of their training. Irregular security forces must have common standards to improve their effectiveness[63] and allow them to operate in harmony with regular forces. This does not mean that all irregular security forces should be the same in each area, but rather that their capabilities, basic skills, and organization should be uniform. Irregular security forces also require strict standards for interacting with the local population to develop trust and gain access to intelligence. Additionally, irregular security forces must be able to report intelligence and changes in the local situation in a timely and accurate manner to enable effective coordination with other forces in the area.

When training irregular forces it is important to remember that they are not American forces. To paraphrase T. E. Lawrence, irregular forces must figure out for themselves the best way to achieve the objectives of the host nation in their local area.[64] Too much influence in tactics and techniques can lead to a dependence on interventionist capabilities that the host nation cannot replicate,[65] thus creating false capacities and hidden weaknesses in the irregular force. David Kilcullen, a contemporary counterinsurgency theorist, reinforces Lawrence's advice to avoid forming irregular security forces in the interventionist's image. Kilcullen advises counterinsurgents to develop irregular security forces that mirror the insurgents' organization, equipment, and mobility.[66]

The task of training irregular security forces is not an easy one, or one that most regular forces are well suited to undertake. As Gardiner wrote, "Regular soldiers could find the *Firqat* infuriating. The SAS, who themselves were somewhat irregular, and were trained to train irregular soldiers, were mostly pretty well adjusted to the task."[67] Recognizing that special operations forces such as the British SAS may not be available to train irregular security forces, at a minimum, the officers employed in training indigenous forces must be highly trained and specially selected for the task.[68]

While highly trained professionals of irregular warfare such as the British SAS may best accomplish training irregular forces, they are not the only option available to counterinsurgents. For example, in 2004 the British Argyll & Sutherland Battalion took on the task of training local security forces in southern Iraq.[69] Partnership of regular counterinsurgent forces comes later in this paper, but it is important to note at this point, however, that in Iraq and more recently in Afghanistan, regular forces work together with indigenous forces of all types with positive results.

Other methods proven effective in building indigenous forces include sending elements of those forces to train in established overseas institutions and combining training programs of both regular and irregular security forces. Corum argues that by sending indigenous forces to overseas training institutions, the host nation creates a more capable professionally trained cadre, those trained overseas return with enhance prestige, and builds stronger bonds between the host nation and the overseas nation sponsoring the training.[70] In Afghanistan, the counterinsurgents train the Afghan National Police alongside the Afghan National Army. This enables a more efficient training program as both forces can train basic skills at the same facilities. Additionally, as the populace views the Afghan National Army as more legitimate than the police due to a history of police corruption, by training these forces together, the counterinsurgents produce a more professional police force.[71]

When counterinsurgents begin to consider developing irregular security forces, they must predicate the training plan on long-term solutions that create viable security institutions. In the early stages of a counterinsurgency campaign, quantity may trump quality. While meeting the immediate security requirements with rapidly raised irregular security forces, counterinsurgents must devise development plans that look to the future in order to incorporate elements of "quantity" forces into the future "quality" forces.[72]

In the Malayan Emergency, the counterinsurgents raised hundreds of thousands of irregular security forces known as Home Guards. Home Guards began as a very basic irregular security force with very few weapons and little to no training. By the end of the campaign, the counterinsurgents developed the Home Guards into a centrally controlled force with common doctrine, improved weapons, and training institutions at the national and state level. The duties performed by the Home Guards increased from basic security guard type duties to augmentation of regular security forces conducting offensive operations.[73]

To retrain irregular security forces either to assume a greater role in the campaign, or to become part of the regular security forces, may require pulling large numbers of forces out of the fight to conduct training. To avoid creating a security vacuum, regular counterinsurgent forces may be required to assume a greater role temporarily while the irregular forces receive additional training. The ability of regular security forces to take on a greater role will influence the speed and scope of irregular security force retraining programs.[74]

Leadership

James Corum noted, "The effectiveness of the indigenous security forces in Cyprus and Malaya was directly related to the quality of the officer leadership."[75] Corum further stated that it is not possible to have effective forces without effective leaders.[76] While developing indigenous security force leaders takes time, the investment is worthwhile to both the host nation and to an interventionist power. The host nation benefits from indigenous security forces with increased capability because of quality leadership. More capable indigenous security forces potentially reduce the requirements for interventionist forces in terms of quantity and duration.[77]

Developing leaders takes time in any security force under the best of conditions. Leader development efforts may take longer depending upon the culture, experience, and education of the pool of potential leadership candidates. Culture can affect leader development in societies that do not reward merit over status. It is important to weigh the cultural implications against westernized ideal leadership characteristics. Recall T.E. Lawrence's advice to allow the locals to develop local solutions. If the irregular security force does not accept "ideal" leader candidates, they become irrelevant at best and can lead to the collapse of the irregular force.

If the pool of candidates has little or no previous military or leadership experience, the task of developing leaders may be more difficult. It may be possible to mitigate the lack of experienced leaders if sufficient development time does not exist. The unclassified version of the 2009 Afghan assessment suggests increased partnership between coalition forces and indigenous forces with poor leadership as a means to minimize the negative effects of poor leadership and to develop those leaders over time.[78]

If literacy rates are low, communication skills poor, or problem-solving capacity low, training leaders becomes a greater challenge. During the counterinsurgency campaign in Dhofar, Oman, the host nation incorporated reading instruction as a component of basic training for the Sultan of Oman's Armed Forces (SAF) to address the low literacy level of the population.[79] Similar education programs for irregular security force leaders could address issues of literacy if needed. Another possible approach would be to provide quality officer leadership from either host nation regular forces or interventionist forces to lead irregular forces temporarily.[80] This approach would allow additional time to train indigenous leadership,[81] but requires acceptance on the part of the local forces and sufficient leadership capacity from the donor force to provide temporary leadership.

Partnership

Partnering regular security forces with irregular security forces has the potential to increase the competence, professionalism, and confidence of irregular security forces. Regular security forces can partner with irregular security forces after they have been formed and trained, or can participate in their formation and development. David Kilcullen suggests starting at the lowest level with platoons building an indigenous squad that becomes a partnered platoon over time. He further suggests that company level leadership should develop the leadership of their indigenous partner.[82]

Historical examples demonstrate the positive effects of partnership while also showing that it is not a panacea. In Vietnam, the United States Marine Corp partnership program known as combined action platoons, or CAPs, was partially successful.[83] As Andrew Krepinevich wrote in *The Army and Vietnam*, "there was a direct correlation between the time a CAP [combined action platoon] stayed in a village and the degree of security achieved, with CAP-protected villages progressing twice as fast as those occupied by the PFs [popular forces] alone."[84] A downside to partnership in Vietnam was the fact that South Vietnamese forces became too much like US forces and relied on American firepower and airpower. When US support dissipated, the South Vietnamese forces collapsed because they had not developed their own solutions within their means.

In Dhofar, British Special Air Service (SAS) troopers partnered with the *firqa* in support of the Sultan of Oman's campaign against communist-backed insurgents. The partnership combined the small unit skills and access to modern military capabilities of the SAS (called British Army Training Teams, or BATTs, during the conflict) with the knowledge of local terrain, ability to communicate with the local population, and understanding of enemy tactics to create a force indispensible to the success of the campaign. According to John Akehurst, commander of the Dhofar Brigade during the conclusion of the Dhofar campaign, "BATT's contribution in raising and training the *Firqats* had been of inestimable importance in the winning of the war."[85] Despite this glowing praise, the SAS/*firqa* combined teams were only part of the forces employed in the strategy to defeat the insurgents, and could not have prevailed alone. As noted by MG Tony Jeapes, "The *firqats'* understanding of ground and their speed of manoeuvre were both superior to SAF troops', but when it came to straight military tactics, the SAF's discipline told every time. The two forces were complementary; neither could have won the war alone."[86]

During Operation Iraqi Freedom, British forces operating in

southern Iraq committed a battalion to train Iraqi forces to conduct counterinsurgency operations based on lessons learned from previous British counterinsurgency experience.[87] The approach included small patrols, limited use of force, and an emphasis on gathering intelligence. The British efforts paid off initially. According to Carter Malkasian, "Some of the first effective Iraqi units appeared in the British operating area."[88] This initial success in developing Iraqi Security Forces in 2003 did not ensure success in southern Iraq. By 2006, British forces had lost control of the area to Shia militias, and had lost the political will to continue in earnest.[89]

<u>Advisory</u>

Advisers can have a great affect on the development of security forces, either positively or negatively. In Dhofar, BATTs advised *firqa* and seconded or contracted British officers were attached to SAF units as commanders. Attaching British officers to Omani units made the SAF more effective. Because the British officers were assigned to the Sultan's forces and under his command, their presence did not overshadow the efforts and leadership of SAF.[90] In contrast, US advisers in Vietnam often stifled the development of Vietnamese commanders. As James Willbanks noted,

> According to one ARVN general, "The power and influence of US advisers in the field did tend to overshadow the role of Vietnamese unit commanders. For example, activities of a unit tended to follow along the lines recommended by the adviser. In many instances, it was the adviser who won the battle by calling effective tactical air or firepower support from US resources. This gradually produced overreliance and sometimes total dependence on US advisers. As a consequence, the initiative, responsibility, and prestige that the unit commander usually wielded were greatly affected and, over the long run, the presence of advisers resulted in reduced opportunity for ARVN cadres to develop their command capabilities and leadership."[91]

Advisers must be able to improve their indigenous partners without overshadowing and undercutting them. Not all good officers and soldiers make good advisers. As Richard Hunt noted regarding advisers in Vietnam,

> John Paul Vann, who would during the course of the war run the CORDS program in III and IV Corps, expected an adviser to become within thirty days of his arrival "the world's leading expert" on the functional and geographical areas of his assignment. At a minimum, Vann expected a district adviser to know in detail the district's political, social, educational, and demographic structure; the local economy; the strengths and effectiveness of all components of friendly and enemy forces; the strengths and weaknesses of local political and military

leaders; the training and equipment of South Vietnamese forces (ARVN to police); the steps being taken to improve those forces; and the location of all friendly, contested, and enemy-controlled hamlets. Vann's list went even further, but he regarded it as representing "only a fraction of the knowledge' an effective district adviser would need to have at his fingertips."[92]

Despite Vann's demands for high-caliber personnel to serve as advisers, the US military did not make the advisory mission in Vietnam a top priority. As Willbanks wrote,

> By early 1970 ... the MACV Training Directorate ... responsible for providing advisers to RVNAF training facilities, was at only 70 percent of assigned strength, and the U.S. training advisory detachments in the field were likewise short-staffed. Another issue was the quality of advisory personnel. ... It was clear that top professionals were not being assigned to training advisory duties.[93]

Those serving as advisers must be dedicated to the task. An example illustrated by Daniel Marston regarding the UK experience in Afghanistan underscores the point that advisory duty should not be an additional duty. He described the 7th Royal Horse Artillery of the 16 Air Assault Brigade. Not only was this artillery unit not trained for advisory duties, it was required to provide indirect fire support while conducting the advisory mission, which resulted in poor performance.[94] Marston described how the British Army changed its approach to better advise their Afghan partners:

> This experience led senior command in the UK to assign a dedicated infantry battalion to train and embed as an OMLT (Operational Mentoring and Liaison Team) in subsequent deployments with the 205 Corps. The subsequent deployments have seen 45 Royal Marines, Grenadier Guards, 2 YORKS, 1 Royal Irish, 1 RIFLES and 2 MERCIANS serving in the OMLT role. ANA actions and reports over the last four years have demonstrated their increased ability.[95]

Finally, those serving as advisers should want to be there among the indigenous troops. Fewer advisers, dedicated to the task and equipped with the requisite skills, will accomplish more than mass levees of the unwilling. As Field Marshal William Slim wrote,

> This I know is rank heresy to many very experienced "coasters."
> I was constantly told that, far from being too many, with the rapidly expanded African forces, more British officers and N.C.O.s were needed. But these large British establishments in African units had great drawbacks. The only way to fill them was to draft officers and N.C.O.s willy-nilly to them, and this did not always give the right kind. The European who

serves with native troops should be, not only much above average in efficiency and character, as he must accept greater responsibility, but he should serve with them because he wants to, because he likes them.[96]

Scope

Scope refers to the size and organization of forces. All of the factors discussed thus far (i.e. purpose, strategy, threat, composition, legitimacy, training, location of employment, leadership, partnership, and advisory) affect the scope of the irregular force. The host nation or intervening power must estimate and refine the scope of irregular security force required to achieve the stated purpose.[97] Should the situation call for a large number of forces, the host nation must weigh quality and quantity, and adjust the training, advisory, partnership, etc. accordingly.

Other factors will likely impact the pace at which the host nation can progress toward attaining a goal of a certain number of irregular security forces. In Dhofar, for example, the expansion of the *firqa* corresponded largely to the progress of SAF across the *jebel*.[98] In Iraq, the expansion of the Sons of Iraq was more rapid, occurring nearly simultaneously in areas across the country.[99] Host nation must start with an estimate of the scope of irregular force requirements. The host nation must then continually revise and update the estimate based on changing conditions in the campaign.

Notes

1.   Department of the Army, U.S. Army Field Manual 1-02 Operational Terms and Graphics, (Washington, DC: Government Printing Office,September 2004), 1-105.

2.   Angel Rabasa, Lesley Anne Warner, Peter Chalk, Ivan Khilko, Paraag Shukla, *Money in the Bank: Lessons Learned from Past Counterinsurgency (COIN) Operations*, (Washington, D.C.:National Defense Research Institute, RAND Corporation, 2007), 13. "The Constabulary was semi-autonomous paramilitary forces set up to fight insurgents. . ." The Philippine Constabulary is not discussed in detail in this paper. For more information on this irregular force, review the RAND study cited above, pages 7-17.

3.   Ian Gardiner, *In the Service of the Sultan: A First Hand Account of the Dhofar Insurgency,* (South Yorkshire, England: Pen & Sword Books Limited, 2007), 156. "The word *firqat* means a military unit or group. The Firqat Forces units were made up of Dhofari Jebeli tribesmen, many of whom had been fighting on the other side but who had been persuaded to come over to the Sultan."

4.   Najim Abed Al-Jabouri and Sterling Jensen, "The Iraqi and AQI Roles in the Sunni Awakening," *PRISM 2*, No. 1 (2010): 3. "The Sons of Iraq program was a U.S.-led and -funded initiative to spread the success of the Anbar Awakening into other Sunni areas, particularly heterogeneous areas, and was not fully supported by the Iraqi government."

5.   References to army include all regular ground forces that are part of the host counterinsurgent military forces. In the US, this would include both Army and Marine forces.

6. Lieutenant Colonel William E. Rieper, *Irregular Forces in Counterinsurgency Operations: Their Roles and Considerations*, (Fort Leavenworth, Kansas: School of Advanced Military Studies, United States Army Command and General Staff College, 2010), 7. "Militias are most useful in security roles closely tied to their homes to safeguard them against insurgent reprisals. Surrogates are quite effective in neighborhood watch programs, occupying checkpoints or access points to markets or other public activities. Their presence reassures civilians and dissuades insurgent attempts to infiltrate population centers. Their actions drive a wedge between the civilian population and the insurgents denying them the opportunity to coerce the population."

7.   Richard Stubbs, "From Search and Destroy to Hearts and Minds: The Evolution of British Strategy in Malaya 1948-60," in *Counterinsurgency in Modern Warfare,* Daniel Marston and Carter Malkasian (eds), (Oxford: Osprey Publishing, 2010), p. 103.

8.   Locally raised and employed security forces provide a great source of human intelligence and create a sense of connection to the government and esprit de corps, as well as employment opportunities within their communities.

9.   James Corum, *Training Indigenous Forces in Counterinsurgency: A Tale of Two Insurgencies.* http://www.strategicstudiesinstitute.army.mil/pubs/ display. cfm?PubID=648, (accessed 13 March 2011): 23. "Though the home guards saw little action in Malaya, they were still of enormous value in suppressing the

insurgency. The home guards were able to assume many routine security duties, freeing up thousands of regular police and military personnel for offensive operations."

10. Police forces include regular "law and order" police, paramilitary police such as the Italian Carabinieri, and intelligence focused police such as the British Special Branch. In the US, there are no equivalents to the Carabinieri (paramilitary) or Special Branch (intelligence gathering) forces. These types of police forces are effective in counterinsurgency campaigns and must not be overlooked when assisting a host nation in developing security forces.

11. Rabasa et al, *Money in the Bank*, 74. "By no means should the military do police work, because the military is trained to capture and kill, whereas the police are trained to detain and interrogate."

12. John Newsinger, *British Counterinsurgency from Palestine to Northern Ireland*, (London: Palgrave, 2002), 48. "Rapid recruitment and the lack of trained police leadership afforded many new policemen the opportunity to abuse their power and use their status to extort money from the population."

13. Rieper, *Irregular Forces in Counterinsurgency Operations,* 45-46. "In each conflict [Malaya, Vietnam, and Operation IRAQI FREEDOM], the irregulars were an excellent source of intelligence, especially the invaluable Human Intelligence on insurgent activities in and around their homes."

14. Corum, *Training Indigenous Forces in Counterinsurgency*, 47. "The Malayan Campaign illustrates the important role irregular, part-time security forces can play in supporting the government campaign. In Malaya, over 200,000 villagers eventually were enrolled and organized into home guard units that served primarily to guard the villages at night. The home guards, with only basic arms and minimal equipment, were very useful in freeing up a large number of regular police and military personnel from basic security and guard duties, which enabled the better-trained and equipped forces to concentrate on the complex operational tasks."

15. Corum, *Training Indigenous Forces in Counterinsurgency*, 35. "Despite political pressure to accomplish a quick fix that would enable the British military to remove forces from Malaya, the Colonial Office had the moral courage to support the long-term strategy proposed by Templer and Young. In Malaya, Templer and Young understood that they were fighting a prolonged war that required a long-term commitment."

16. Brian Linn, *The Philippine War, 1899-1902*. (Lawrence: University of Kansas Press, 2000), 204. General Arthur MacArthur, the commanding officer beginning in 1900, issued General Order 87 which directed the arming of the police and creation of mounted constabulary bodies for operations within the boundaries of towns and barrios. In December of 1900, with the imminent departure of US volunteers, MacArthur ordered the arming of these forces and transferred much of the pacification duties to them. "...[I]n 1901 local police [constabularies] proved some of the more effective counterinsurgency forces the army raised."

17. Corum, *Training Indigenous Forces in Counterinsurgency*, 47. "Templer took an eclectic mix of loosely-organized local forces and quietly instituted some centralized control and supervision. He brought in a team of experience

officers and set up district and state home guard organization with a small training center in each state. The central home guard command issued doctrine, provided training guidance, and set standards. The state and district commands ensured that some rudimentary training was provided, and that local commands performed to standard."

18. Rieper, *Irregular Forces in Counterinsurgency Operations,* 37. "The most glaring weakness in the program was its failure to develop a coherent plan to transition SOIs after they had secured the environment ... What the SOIs wanted was inclusion in the ISF, which GOI resisted."

19. Robert Komer, *The Malayan Emergency in Retrospect: Organization of a Successful Counterinsurgency Effort.* (Santa Monica: RAND, 1972), 39. "Gradually the local security force in each Chinese village came to be a police post of ten to twelve Malay constables, supported by a part-time Home Guard of about thirty-five men, of whom normally five were on duty patrolling the perimeter at night..."

20. Population control measures include census taking, controlling access to secured population centers, curfew enforcement, rationing commodities, and searching persons, dwellings, and vehicles for contraband.

21. Fixed security points include traffic control points (both vehicular and foot traffic), securing critical infrastructure, and other static guard duties.

22. Rieper, *Irregular Forces in Counterinsurgency Operations*, 51 "Sponsors [e.g. host nation or intervening power in support of the host nation] should note that militias could falter if left unsupported and conventional forces should closely monitor their activities to ensure compliance."

23. Stubbs, "From Search and Destroy to Hearts and Minds," 106. Lieutenant General Briggs took over the campaign in Malaya in 1950 with a plan to "dominate the populated areas" and build up "a feeling of complete security" so that people would provide the government with information about the communists, break up the Min Yuen and thereby isolate the MRLA from their supplies of food and information, and force the MRLA to attack 'us on our own ground.'"

24. Corum, *Training Indigenous Forces in Counterinsurgency*, 13. "The massive application of largely untrained manpower worked to stabilize the situation. Despite an overwhelming advantage in manpower and resources, this policy made no headway. Indeed, the insurgency continued to grow, with the active insurgent military force reaching its peak of 8,000 in 1951."

25. Raymond A. Millen, "Time for a Strategic and Intellectual Pause in Afghanistan," *Parameters* 40, No. 2 (Summer 2010): 38. "Worse, the corresponding rapid increase of the Afghan National Army (ANA) to 134,000 soldiers (and perhaps 240,000) as part of an exit strategy lacks a logical rationale."

26. Corum, *Training Indigenous Forces in Counterinsurgency*, 18-19. The police force in Malaya was cut by 10,000 between 1952 and 1953 in order to shed those police who were corrupt or incompetent.

27. Corum, *Training Indigenous Forces in Counterinsurgency*, 39-40.

28. David Galula, *Counterinsurgency Warfare Theory and Practice.* (Florida: Hailer, 2005), 24.

29. Galula, *Counterinsurgency Warfare Theory and Practice*, 24-25. "Allowing one platoon for every hamlet, 400,000 men would have been required for the static forces. Fifty thousand were needed for the mobile reserves, taking into account the threat posed by the borders. Seventy thousand were required to protect the six or seven thousand vulnerable points. The total bill came to 520,000 men, not counting the support services and the Navy and Air Force. Not until August 1956 did we reach our greatest strength, and that was only 400,000 men. The rest clearly would have to be provided by the population itself, but not before we could get the people to commit themselves on our side. This in turn required that we first give them security, which we could not provide because we were understrength. We were apparently caught in a vicious circle from which only strategy could free us."

30. Galula, *Counterinsurgency Warfare Theory and Practice*, 72-73.

31. Robert Komer, *Bureaucracy at War: U.S. Performance in the Vietnam Conflict.* (Boulder, CO: Westview Press, 1986), 135. Assistant Secretary Roger Hilsman's final memorandum to the Secretary of State in March 1964 called for, "primary emphasis on giving security to the villagers. The tactics are the so-called oil-blot approach, starting with a secure area and extending it slowly...This calls for the use of military forces in a different way from that of orthodox, conventional war. Rather that chasing Viet Cong, the military must put primary emphasis on clear-and-hold operations and on rapid reinforcement of villages under attack. It is also important of course, to keep the Viet Cong regular units off balance by conventional offensive operations, but these should be secondary to the major task of extending security..."

32. This is an oversimplification of the strategy which was intended to attack the insurgent network and organization versus the insurgent forces. For a complete discussion of the French strategy in Algeria, see David Galula, Counterinsurgency Warfare Theory and Practice, *Pacification in Algeria 1956-1958.* Santa Monica: RAND, 2006, pp. 5-25 and 243-270; and Roger Trinquier, *Modern Warfare: A French View of Counterinsurgency.* Ft Leavenworth: CSI, 1985, pp. 67-93.

33. Force protection can include barriers or berms to provide cover or to make approach by vehicle difficult, and personal equipment such as body armor and helmets.

34. British Army Tactical Doctrine Retrieval Cell, "CSAF Assessment in Dhofar," (Oman: CSAF, 16 Feb. 1972), 11. "There will be major problems to overcome in respect of resupply, casualty evacuation and morale, but I believe that the reduced visibility will offer great opportunities for offensive action to the side which is the best trained and most aggressive. Firqats supported by 22 SAS should achieve a lot: Firqats supported by a small party from SAF or unsupported will achieve little. They might even decamp to the Coastal Plain. Thus I recommend that 22 SAS be permitted to remain in Dhofar at one Squadron strength until at least the end of the monsoon, with the primary task of supporting the Firqats on the Jebel in the Eastern Area."

35. Andrew F. Krepinevich, Jr., *The Army and Vietnam*, (Maryland: The John Hopkins University Press, 1986), 13. "Paramilitary forces should be drawn from among the inhabitants and trained in counterinsurgency operations such as small unit patrolling, night operations, and the ambush."

36. Corum, *Training Indigenous Forces in Counterinsurgency*, 11. "At the start of the insurgency, the police faced other daunting problems that severely limited their ability to collect intelligence. There were very few police personnel of Chinese ethnic background, and almost no Malayan or British intelligence personnel who knew Chinese. This greatly limited the amount and quality of intelligence that the police could collect on the insurgents..."

37. Rabasa et al, *Money in the Bank*, 74. "In recruiting indigenous security forces, the counterinsurgents should seek to create a force that reflects the ethnic, religious, and socioeconomic makeup of the local population and should make a special effort to recruit a reasonable number of potentially oppressed ethnic minorities to increase their stake in fighting the insurgency."

38. Colonel Richard Iron, *Britain's Longest War: Northern Ireland 1967-2007,* in Daniel Marston and Carter Malkasian (eds.), *Counterinsurgency in Modern Warfare*. Oxford: Osprey Publishing, 2010, p. 158. "By mid-1970, the great majority of the Catholic minority saw itself under attack not just from the Protestant majority but from the British Army as well. Recruitment into the newly formed PIRA grew dramatically."

39. Najim and Jensen, "The Iraqi and AQI Roles in the Sunni Awakening," 13-14.

40. Rieper, *Irregular Forces in Counterinsurgency Operations*, ii. "Militias also provide a means for the government to garner local support against the insurgency through inclusion. They can facilitate reconciliation with disaffected groups and provide a unifying force for these groups in politics."

41. Corum, *Training Indigenous Forces in Counterinsurgency*, 23. "As the security forces became more representative of the population, the attitude of the Chinese population towards the government became more positive."

42. Galula, *Counterinsurgency Warfare Theory and Practice*, 57.

43. Corum, *Training Indigenous Forces in Counterinsurgency*, 23. "Moreover, recruiting the Chinese into the home guard had the very positive political effect of bringing a large number of the Chinese into the government process and making them part of the solution to the insurgency."

44. Rabasa et al, *Money in the Bank*, 72.

45. Carter Malkasian, *The Role of Perceptions and Political reform in Counterinsurgency: The Case of Western Iraq, 2004-2005, Small Wars and Insurgencies*, Vol. 17, no 3, September 2006, p. 384. "Some insurgents feared to operate within the city because the tight security environment allowed people to inform on them with little fear of retribution."

46. Malkasian, *The Role of Perceptions and Political reform in Counterinsurgency*, 383-384. "The insurgents could no longer mount major attacks, such as assaulting police stations or conducting car bombings, to impress the population of their strength. People interacted with Iraqi and Coalition forces freely."

47 . Corum, *Training Indigenous Forces in Counterinsurgency*, 48. "When a nation is faced with instability and disorder, there is an inevitable response for local citizens to establish militias and irregular forces for their own security. It

is politically unwise, perhaps even impossible, for any national government to ignore the issue of local militias, which are based on the natural desire for local security."

48. Corum, *Training Indigenous Forces in Counterinsurgency*, 1. "Success in counterinsurgency depends on a number of major elements, to include establishing the legitimacy of the government in the eyes of the people, defeating the insurgent forces, providing a basic level of security for the population, and creating the conditions for economic growth. Underpinning these tasks is the establishment of an effective security force."

49. Sir Robert Thompson, *Defeating Communist Insurgency: The Lessons of Malaya and Vietnam*, (New York: Frederick Praeger, 1967),19.

50. Gardiner, *In the Service of the Sultan*, 156. "It must also be said that many Jebelis recognized the Sultan had won their hearts and minds by removing the causes of their original rebellion, and by meeting more closely their needs and aspirations. But perhaps the greatest incentive was that most human of instincts, the wish to be on the winning side when the war stopped. There could be no more unambiguous indicator that the Sultan was winning than the flow of these people to his side."

51. Civil Aid Teams were developed to bring the benefits of governance to disaffected areas in order to tie the community to the Sultan, gather intelligence, and address the underlying grievances of Dhofaris.

52. Gardiner, *In the Service of the Sultan*, 159. "...the concept of recruiting the Firqat and keeping them alongside was a courageous masterstroke, generally attributed to John Watts in 1970 when he was the Commanding Officer of the SAS ... It started with the placing of Civil Aid Teams with medics in the towns of Taqa and Mirbat. They treated all-comers but mostly the women and children. As the miracle of penicillin gradually banished hitherto chronic afflictions, the word began to spread to the men folk on the *jebel*. They too would come in with their ailments, and so on; and thus the tide of war had imperceptibly but indubitably turned."

53. Gardiner, *In the Service of the Sultan*, 159. "Hitherto, there had been virtually no Dhofaris in the Army, and the Sultan's forces in Dhofar had looked suspiciously like an army of occupation. By bringing the Jebelis on board in substantial numbers in the form of Firqats, that could no longer be said."

54. Gardiner, *In the Service of the Sultan*, 157. "They were supplied and paid like any other military formation. It was best not to be too rigorous with the arithmetic when counting them as there were always ghosts on the payroll and it was not easy to see what the Sultan was getting for his money. They were intensely tribal and would only work in their own tribal area and so, to the orderly military eye, they had limited utility."

55. Gardiner, *In the Service of the Sultan*, 159. "As our former enemies they knew the ground and the tactics of their former friends intimately, and they were good at things that we were poor at, namely reconnaissance, gathering intelligence and communicating with the nomadic population. They were of that population, after all. They were, therefore, extremely useful in retaining the peace in an area which had been cleared of *adoo*, thereby leaving conventional forces to get on

with prosecuting the war elsewhere."

56. Gardiner, *In the Service of the Sultan*, 159.

57. Galula, *Counterinsurgency Warfare Theory and Practice*, 79. "The operations needed to relieve the population from the insurgent's threat and to convince it that the counterinsurgent will ultimately win are necessarily of an intensive nature and of long duration. They require a large concentration of efforts, resources, and personnel. This means that the efforts cannot be diluted all over the country but must be applied successively area by area."

58. Galula, *Counterinsurgency Warfare Theory and Practice*, 97. "According to the first approach, one proceeds from the difficult to the easy. …It is the fastest way, if it succeeds. The other approach, from the easy to the difficult, requires fewer means at the outset, but is slower and gives more opportunity for the insurgent to develop and to consolidate … The choice between the approaches depends essentially on the relative strength of the opponents."

59. General Chang Tien-chen, Chief of the South China Service Corps, member of the Central Committee, as quoted in *The New York Times*, 4 July 1949: "A revolutionary war is 20 per cent military action and 80 per cent political."

60. Jeffrey Race, *War Comes to Long An.* (California: UC Press, 1972), 164.

61. Daniel Marston, "Realizing the Extent of Our Errors and Forging the Road Ahead Afghanistan 2001-2010," in *Counterinsurgency in Modern Warfare,* (eds.) Daniel Marston and Carter Malkasian, (Oxford: Osprey Publishing, 2010), 271.

62. FM 3-24 Counterinsurgency, 6-16.

63. Corum, *Training Indigenous Forces in Counterinsurgency*, 47. "The central home guard command issued doctrine, provided training guidance, and set standards. The state and district commands ensured that some rudimentary training was provided, and that local commands performed to standard. The efficiency of the home guards was improved without sacrificing their local character."

64. Lieutenant Colonel T. E. Lawrence, "Twenty-Seven Articles," *The Arab Bulletin*, Article Number 8, 27 August 1917. "Do not try to do too much with your own hands. Better the Arabs do it tolerably than that you do it perfectly. It is their war, and you are to help them, not to win it for them."

65. James Willbanks, *Abandoning Vietnam.* (Lawrence, Kansas: University of Kansas Press, 2004), 281. "In many instances, it was the adviser who won the battle by calling effective tactical air or firepower support from US resources. This gradually produced overreliance and sometimes total dependence on US advisers."

66. Lieutenant Colonel David Kilcullen, "Twenty-Eight Articles," *Military Review*, May-June 2006, 107. Article 22 states, "The natural tendency is to build forces in the U.S. image, with the aim of eventually handing our role over to them. This is a mistake. Instead, local indigenous forces need to mirror the enemy's capabilities and seek to supplant the insurgent's role."

67. Gardiner, *In the Service of the Sultan*, 156.

68. Ian Beckett, "The British Counter-insurgency Campaign in Dhofar,

1965-1975," *Counterinsurgency in Modern Warfare*. Daniel Marston and Carter Malkasian (eds.), (Oxford: Osprey Publishing, 2010), 186.

69.   Carter Malkasian, "Counterinsurgency in Iraq," *Counterinsurgency in Modern Warfare*. Daniel Marston and Carter Malkasian (eds.), (Oxford: Osprey Publishing, 2010), 290.

70.   Corum, *Training Indigenous Forces in Counterinsurgency*, 44.

71.   David Barno, "Fighting the other war: counterinsurgency strategy in Afghanistan 2003-2005." *Military Review*, 87:5, September-October 2007, 39.

72.   Corum, *Training Indigenous Forces in Counterinsurgency*, 39. "While it might be necessary to stand up ad hoc security forces at the start of an emergency, U.S. policy should be to institute a comprehensive program of police and security training as quickly as possible ... should have a comprehensive plan for police training before intervention begins, as well as ample funds and specialist personnel allocated for the task ... [envisioning] a several-year program to systematically build police institutions and leadership."

73.   Corum, *Training Indigenous Forces in Counterinsurgency*, 47-48.

74.   Corum, *Training Indigenous Forces in Counterinsurgency*, 43.

75.   Corum, *Training Indigenous Forces in Counterinsurgency*, 42.

76.   Corum, *Training Indigenous Forces in Counterinsurgency*, 42.

77.   Corum, *Training Indigenous Forces in Counterinsurgency*, 44.

78.   General Stanley McCrystal, COMISAF Initial Assessment (UNCLASSIFIED), (Kabul, Afghanistan: Headquarters International Security Assistance Force, 30 August 2009), G-2

79.   Walter Ladwig III, *Supporting Allies in COIN: Britain and the Dhofar Rebellion,* Small Wars and Insurgencies, Vol. 19:1, March 2008, p. 72.

80.   Ladwig, *Supporting Allies in COIN*, 71. "...the British provided assistance in four key areas: developing a plan for victory; training and expanding the Sultan's Armed Forces; providing experienced leadership and technical skills; and equipping the SAF for counterinsurgency."

81.   Beckett, "The British Counter-insurgency Campaign in Dhofar," 185.

82.   Kilcullen, "Twenty-Eight Articles", 107. Article 22 states, "Platoons should aim to train one local squad, then use that squad as a nucleus for a partner platoon. Company headquarters should train an indigenous leadership team."

83.   See Michael Hennessy, *Strategy in Vietnam: The Marines and Revolutionary Warfare in I Corps, 1965-1972*, (Westport, Ct: Praeger, 1997) for more details on CAPs.

84.   Krepinevich, *The Army and Vietnam*, 174.

85.   John Akehurst, *We Won a War, The Campaign in Oman 1965-1975*, (Great Britain: Biddles Ltd., 1982), 177.

86.   Tony Jeapes, *SAS: Secret War,* (Surrey: Harper Collins, 1996), 237.

87.   Malkasian, "Counterinsurgency in Iraq," 290. "Applying the lessons of a half-century of counterinsurgency, the British patrolled in small units, rigorously

collected intelligence, and used firepower sparingly. ... As early as September 2003, British generals made the development of local Iraqi forces a priority. For example, in 2004, the entire Argyll & Sutherland Battalion was dedicated to training them."

88. Malkasian, "Counterinsurgency in Iraq," 290.

89. Malkasian, "Counterinsurgency in Iraq," 306.

90. Ladwig, *Supporting Allies in COIN*, 79. "Attaching officers directly to the host nation's service provides an alternative to the standard 'advisor model.' ... Making themselves part of the SAF's force structure, and therefore ultimately under the Sultan's command, sent a strong message to Omanis that the government in Muscat, not London, was calling the shots."

91. Willbanks, *Abandoning Vietnam*, 281. "Buu Vien, a close personal adviser to President Thieu, said after the war: 'The presence of American advisers at all levels of the military hierarchy created among the Vietnamese leadership a mentality of reliance on their advice and suggestions.'... According to one ARVN general, ... 'The power and influence of US advisers in the field did tend to overshadow the role of Vietnamese unit commanders. For example, activities of a unit tended to follow along the lines recommended by the adviser. In many instances, it was the adviser who won the battle by calling effective tactical air or firepower support from US resources. This gradually produced overreliance and sometimes total dependence on US advisers. As a consequence, the initiative, responsibility, and prestige that the unit commander usually wielded were greatly affected and, over the long run, the presence of advisers resulted in reduced opportunity for ARVN cadres to develop their command capabilities and leadership.'"

92. Richard Hunt, *Pacification: The American Struggle for Vietnam's Hearts and Minds*. (Colorado: Westview Press, 1995), 94-95.

93. Willbanks, *Abandoning Vietnam*, 37. "By early 1970, the U.S. authorities were so disturbed by the situation [the state of training in GVN forces] that the army chief of staff dispatched a fact-finding team led by Brig. Gen. Donnelly Bolton to tour RVNAF training facilities in Vietnam...Bolton's team found the efforts of both the South Vietnamese and the U.S. military training advisers in Vietnam to be insufficient...the MACV Training Directorate ... responsible for providing advisers to RVNAF training facilities, was at only 70 percent of assigned strength, and the U.S. training advisory detachments in the field were likewise short-staffed. Another issue was the quality of advisory personnel ... It was clear that top professionals were not being assigned to training advisory duties."

94. Daniel Marston, "Realizing the extent of our errors and forging the road ahead: Afghanistan 2001-2010," in Daniel Marston and Carter Malkasian (eds.), *Counterinsurgency in Modern Warfare*. Oxford: Osprey Publishing, 2010, p. 281."One key aspect of the campaign in Helmand (as in the rest of Afghanistan) is the establishment of a viable indigenous security apparatus. The British were assigned to work with the 3/205 Kandak on *Herrick IV*. Initially, due to the paucity of troops on the first operational tour, the 16 Air Assault Brigade could only assign their artillery detachment, 7th Royal Horse Artillery, as advisers to the Kandak,

something they had not been trained for. Hence there was much scrambling to get systems up and running. It must be remembered that this regiment, in addition to fulfilling this role, was also providing artillery support for the brigade during the deployment. They did their best, but it is evident that execution of the mission was more or less ad hoc."

95. Daniel Marston, "Realizing the extent of our errors and forging the road ahead: Afghanistan 2001-2010," in Daniel Marston and Carter Malkasian (eds.), *Counterinsurgency in Modern Warfare*. Oxford: Osprey Publishing, 2010, p. 281.

96. William Slim, Viscount, *Defeat into Victory*, (London: MacMillan Publisher Limited, 1986), 166.

97. Factors that help estimate the appropriate size include the capabilities of the enemy, the area of employment (e.g. number of areas to secure, the dispersion of these areas, and terrain), a reasonable projection of the capabilities of the irregular security forces, and the overall strategy of the campaign.

98. See Chapter Three for a discussion of the *firqa* in Dhofar.

99. See Chapter Four for a discussion of the Sons of Iraq.

Chapter 3
Dhofar Case Study

The officers whom Britain sent to Oman, both contracted and regular, were highly trained volunteers. ... The patience and tolerance to live harmoniously in an unfamiliar culture; the fortitude to be content with less than comfortable circumstances for prolonged periods; and understanding of and sympathy for a foreign history and religion; a willingness to learn a new language; the flexibility, imagination and humility necessary to climb into the head of the people who live by a very different set of assumptions; none of these are to be found automatically in our modern developed Euro-Atlantic culture.

— Ian Beckett,
"The British Counter-insurgency Campaign in Dhofar"

The campaign in Dhofar from 1965 to 1975 is widely considered a successful execution of counterinsurgency warfare.[1] Lieutenant Colonel John McKeown captured the significance of the victory in his dissertation on the campaign: "It was a rare victory in a period when the combination of real grievance and Communist exploitation of it proved irresistible in many countries with vastly greater Western support."[2] What is not as widely understood are the reasons for success in Oman against a well-organized and equipped insurgency which enjoyed strong popular support.

Just as there were several factors which contributed to the insurgency, there were several factors which contributed to its defeat. In his book *We Won a War*, John Akehurst described what he believed to be the reasons for the Sultan of Oman's victory over the insurgents.[3] Chief among these was winning the support of the population. In Oman this support manifested in the form of fighters changing sides to support the Sultan of Oman against their former insurgent comrades. While Sultan Said bin Taimur nearly lost the campaign due to his alienation of the population, his son, Sultan Qaboos bin Said, quickly turned the war around and won decisively once he had the population on his side. Ian Gardiner captured this sentiment succinctly: "It must also be said that many Jebelis recognized the Sultan had won their hearts and minds by removing the causes of their original rebellion, and by meeting more closely their needs and aspirations. ... There could be no more unambiguous indicator that the Sultan was winning than the flow of these people to his side."[4] The flow of people to the side of the Sultan, to fight for the Sultan against the remaining insurgents, is one of the unique aspects of the campaign in Oman, and relates most directly to the topic of this research, irregular security forces.

Known as *firqa*, the fighters that joined the Sultan against their former comrades turned the tide against the insurgents in many ways. Their shift in allegiance resulted in a large change in the balance of power in the Sultan's favor. By gaining the support of the former enemy fighters, the Sultan also gained the support of the families and tribes of those fighters which helped reduce insurgent support and freedom of maneuver. Although the *firqa* had weaknesses as a fighting force, their strengths compensated for the weaknesses of the Sultan's conventional forces, known as the Sultan's Armed Forces or SAF, and vice versa. While both the *firqa* and the SAF each played vital roles in the campaign, neither would likely have won without the other.

Background

The Sultanate of Oman is on the southern end of the Arabian Peninsula along the coast of the Arabian Sea. Oman is roughly the size of England and Wales combined.[5] Adjacent to Oman are Yemen to the west, Saudi Arabia and the United Arab Emirates to the north, and across the Strait of Hormuz, Iran. Although at the time of the insurgency that began in 1965 Oman had no significant oil production, its location at the mouth of the Strait of Hormuz was of strategic interest based on the flow of oil to the west and Japan through the strait.[6]

The Sultan of Oman rules Oman as a patrimonial monarchy.[7] Sultan Said bin Taimur ruled Oman at the outset of the 1965-1975 insurgency, followed by his son Qaboos who deposed Sultan Said and became Sultan of Oman on 23 July 1970. Sultan Qaboos bin Said rules Oman to the present day.

Dhofar is a region within the Sultanate of Oman, and is geographically[8] and ethnically[9] divided from the rest of the nation. Dhofaris are distinct from other Omanis due to their physical features and language which more closely resemble East Africans than Arabs.[10] Under Sultan Said Bin Taimur, most Omanis viewed Dhofaris as inferior even though the Sultan's wife was Dhofari and his son Qaboos was half Dhofari.[11] A common saying among Northern Omanis was, "If your path is blocked by a snake and a Dhofari, kill the Dhofari first."[12] While the origin of this saying is unknown, it may have come from the numerous rebellions in Dhofar since the Sultan of Oman annexed Dhofar in 1879.[13]

Dhofar itself is internally divided by geography and ethnicity. Geographically, Dhofar consists mainly of a coastal plain and a high plateau known as the Jebel. The Jebelis, the peoples who occupy the Jebel, are nomadic cattle herdsmen with a distinct dialect "closer to Aramaic than Arabic."[14] The Jebel runs west to east just north of Oman's coastal plain in the western part of the country. South of the Jebel is the Salalah plain between the Jebel and the Arabian Sea. North of the Jebel lies a vast expanse of open desert of sand and gravel. For most of the year the Jebel is barren, but during the monsoon season it becomes green with vegetation and is covered in a heavy low-lying fog.

Prelude to War

In 1959, the Sultan of Oman defeated an uprising that was spawned from strife between the Sultan of Oman and the Imam of the Interior. The campaign unfolded on the Jebel Akhdar, which means Green Mountain, in the northern part of Oman.[15] Prior to the rebellion, Saudi Arabia claimed much of Omani territory and occupied portions of it, most likely motivated by the discovery of oil.[16] The Sultan's Armed Forces (SAF), commanded by seconded and contracted British officers, was born of an agreement made in 1958 between Sultan Said and the Parliamentary Under-Secretary of State at the Foreign Office in the British Government, Julian Amery.[17] In addition to this beneficial arrangement, Britain sent SAS forces to Oman to support the Sultan in defeating the insurgents in what came to be referred to as the Jebel Akdar, or "Green Mountain," campaign.[18]

Sultan Said Bin Taimur attempted to preserve and protect traditional Omani society from corrupting western influences by banning not only education, modern medicine, internal and external migration, and technology, but also trousers, smoking, eyeglasses, bicycles, and many other vestiges of modern society.[19] Sultan Said bin Taimur misguidedly believed that he could shield Dhofari culture from external corrupting influences.[20] He made no exceptions in his policies, and confined his son Qaboos to house arrest upon his return from the British Royal Military Academy at Sandhurst[21] and a tour in Germany with the British Army's Cameronians.[22] Sultan Said also remained reclusive himself[23] and effectively isolated himself from his people.

Additionally, the sultan refused to invest in developing the country until he had cash in hand from oil production. While it was apparent that Oman would soon profit from the discovery of oil, Sultan Said was unwilling to borrow money against future profits as he believed this was against the teachings of the Quran.[24] Sultan Said's reluctance to invest in improving infrastructure combined with repressive edicts meant to protect Oman from western corruption resulted in rebellion among the Dhofari tribes who were hardest hit by Sultan Said's policies.

1963-1969

The Sultan of Oman and the SAF battled an insurgency from 1965 to 1975 that began with dissatisfaction among Dhofaris over the repressive edicts of the Sultan,[25] and the fact that Dhofaris were mistrusted and mistreated by the Sultan and by many within Oman. The roots of the insurgency formed in 1962 with the creation of the Dhofar Charitable Association (DCA) by disaffected members of the Arab Nationalist Movement (ANM) in Dhofar. While the DCA's claimed purpose was to improve the lot of Dhofaris, its true purpose was to prepare for an uprising against the British-backed Sultanate in Oman.[26] The DCA formed the roots of the organization that would eventually oppose Sultan Said known as the Dhofar Liberation Front (DLF).[27]

The uprising began in 1963 with attacks led by Musselim bin Nufl, formerly in the employment of the Sultan. These attacks were made against a relatively soft target consisting of some assets of a foreign oil company and resulted in several vehicles destroyed and one of the Sultan's *askars* (guards) killed. Nufl fled to Saudi Arabia and then to Iraq where he trained in guerilla warfare and gathered others to return to fight against the Sultan. Nufl's group incorporated other dissident groups to include the ANM, the DCA, and members of the Dhofar Soldiers' Organization[28] to form the core of the DLF in 1964.[29] The members of these opposition groups were generically referred to as *adoo*, a Dhofari term adopted by the British forces during the campaign.

Because the Sultan offered no terms to negotiate a settlement or address grievances, and no hope of amnesty, the only way to end the fighting was for one side to destroy the other. In fact, in 1966, Colonel Anthony Lewis, Commander of SAF, felt the war was stalemated and recommended increased military pressure paired with political concessions to break the stalemate.[30] In his dissertation on the Dhofar campaign published in 1981, McKeown quotes from the Colonel Lewis' paper: "Rebel movements have only been finally destroyed by leniency. A rebel who has no prospect of surrender terms will fight to the bitter end once he is committed to the movement. If there is some opportunity of pardon, this thought when his morale is low will weaken his resistance and lead him to capitulate."[31] According to a former senior intelligence officer at the time, many of the people and sheikhs on the jebel felt the conflict would have ended in late '66 or early '67 had Sultan Said offered reasonable terms.[32]

The DLF began to receive support in the form of Soviet and Chinese weaponry, and an influx of ideological rebels. Both the materiel and personnel came through Yemen, then a communist-supported safe haven created in part due to the withdrawal of British forces. The influx of new ideologues supplanted the DLF leadership.[33] In 1968 the DLF held its second conference where communist hardliners took control.[34] DLF then changed its name to the Popular Front for the Liberation of the Occupied Arabian Gulf, or PFLOAG.[35] PFLOAG's ideology was Marxist versus DLF's nationalist ideology.[36] Ian Beckett described the *adoo* gain in strength under PFLOAG:

> Its new manifesto called for the breaking of tribalism, the end of Western imperialism and the institution of a Marxist republic. With an estimated hard core of 2,000 active insurgents in the People's Liberation Army (PLA), dedicated death-squads known as idaarat, and 3,000 part-time jebali militia, PFLOAG had become a formidable opponent. It comfortably

outnumbered the single battalion of the SAF now stationed in Dhofar.[37]

While the SAF had some tactical success, no meaningful progress could be obtained due to the sultan's firm stance against concessions. PFLOAG increased its activity resulting in a rise in contacts with SAF from about one per week to several per day. This increased pressure caused SAF to abandon western Dhofar and cede control of lines of communication and the population to PFLOAG.[38]

From 1964 to 1969, the Sultan's efforts to defeat the insurgency struggled to make any meaningful progress. The SAF consisted of three battalions of infantry consisting primarily of Baluchi recruits, with some supporting personnel (e.g. armored cars, artillery). These units were led by seconded or contracted British officers, but had no familiarity with the Dhofar region, nor any connection with the Dhofari peoples, and were seen as a foreign army by the Dhofaris.[39] In essence, Sultan Said was attempting to counter a foreign-backed insurgency fueled by legitimate grievances in a geographically and ethnically separated part of his country with a small force comprised of foreign troops unfamiliar with the terrain or the people of Dhofar, and unable to hold ground in the contested area.

In addition to the advantage of knowledge of the local terrain and population, examination of past campaigns indicate several other advantages of recruiting forces from within the contested area. Commenting on operations in Vietnam, noted author Andrew Krepinevich advised, "Paramilitary forces should be drawn from among the inhabitants and trained in counterinsurgency operations such as small unit patrolling, night operations, and the ambush."[40] The lack of forces with an understanding of the local area negatively impacts intelligence collection as noted by James Corum in his examination of the Malayan Emergency: "There were very few police personnel of Chinese ethnic background, and almost no Malayan or British intelligence personnel who knew Chinese. This greatly limited the amount and quality of intelligence that the police could collect on the insurgents…"[41] Finally, possibly of greatest importance, local recruiting contributes to representative security forces that are more legitimate in the eyes of the local population.[42] As representative recruiting in local areas includes all ethnic, religious, and tribal groups, it creates ties between the government and all of the people.[43]

The Sultan's small force, unfamiliar and unconnected to the population, had no ability to retain any ground taken from the *adoo*.[44] In fact, most of the incursions into Dhofar by SAF from '64 to '69 were short-term raids aimed at killing or capturing *adoo*.[45] During the monsoon season, SAF would withdraw from the jebel entirely.

Although many of the SAF's difficulties stemmed from its lack of resources, the *adoo* fighters they faced were a formidable and capable force. Tony Jeapes, an SAS commander during the campaign, described the *adoo*'s capabilities:

> They were good fighters, that I certainly knew. They had cleared SAF off the jebel and it was over a year since SAF had spent more than 24 hours up there. . . I had plenty of evidence as to the *adoo's* fighting capability. They were brave men, not afraid to push home an attack if SAF made a blunder. They were skillful at using ground to provide covered approaches and their brown skins and dull clothing gave them natural camouflage. Whereas the SAF tended to stay in one place, the *adoo* were constantly moving, probing the SAF flanks, working around them to cut off their withdrawal, and using every dip and fold of the ground to advantage.[46]

Additionally, the *adoo* knew the terrain and how to maximize it in conducting ambushes and sniping attacks. The *adoo* had great mobility which they used to their advantage against the Sultan's force which was less mobile and tended to try to hold ground. The *adoo* were well equipped, but often poorly trained resulting in inconsistent results with mortars and recoilless rifles. Using traditional tactics of the guerilla facing a stronger conventional force, the *adoo* sought to use hit-and-run tactics to harass and wear down the SAF.[47]

Insurgent gains against the Sultan's forces included control over most of the jebel by 1969. The coastal town of Rakhyut and the Thumrait road fell to the insurgents.[48] By the end of 1969, there were no SAF operating in the western part of Dhofar.[49] The assessment of the situation during the 1969 monsoon was that "SAF could hold Salalah and contain the enemy, but not suppress them."[50]

To further complicate matters, the Sultan required a contingent of his troops, at least one full battalion,[51] to remain in Northern Oman to conduct training, prepare for future rotations in Dhofar, and keep the peace.[52] While this may seem an excessive demand for forces away from the fight in Dhofar, the threat of attack in Northern Oman was real.[53]

1970

The long-dreaded threat of attack in Northern Oman became reality in June of 1970 when a group of rebel leaders attacked the military encampments at Ziki and Nizwa.[54] The attack on Ziki was intended to allow the rebel leaders to gain experience which they would take back to their separate groups. Each group would then conduct attacks against predetermined military and civil targets in Northern Oman. The attack was a success in the fact that all of the leaders gained experience and walked away unharmed. Unfortunately for the *adoo* leaders, the SAF Commander at Ziki pursued them and killed or captured the lot, thus decimating the leadership of the insurgency in the north.[55]

Although the uprising in Northern Oman was quickly crushed, the fact that it happened at all underscored the level of dissatisfaction of Omanis with the Sultan who still refused to change his policies, made only minor investments in his armed forces, and showed no signs of altering his course.[56] As Walter Ladwig III states in his examination of the conflict, "By 1970 it had become clear to London that Sultan Said was an obstacle to victory in Dhofar . . . At the same time, it was recognized that no change of government would occur without the acquiescence of the British officers seconded to the Sultan's service."[57] Sultan Said had to go.

Sultan Qaboos overthrew his father in a largely bloodless palace coup on 23 July 1970.[58] Although the exact details remain unclear, Sultan Qaboos obviously had some assistance from the British government. Indeed, at the time of the coup, a British Royal Air Force transport aircraft happened to be parked at RAF Salalah and was used to transport the deposed Sultan Said out of Oman. It was the only time such an aircraft was seen at RAF Salalah during the course of the war.[59]

Sultan Qaboos wasted no time. Soon after deposing his father, he enacted a series of broad reforms aimed at addressing the grievances which fueled the insurgency as well as modernizing and increasing the size of the armed forces. He recalled Omani exiles that were unable to return previously due to his father's policies against migration. Among those recalled was Sultan Qaboos' uncle, Tariq bin Taimur, who Qaboos made the prime minister. Other reforms included the release of political prisoners, lifting bans on internal movement and travel between Oman and certain foreign countries, and creation of four new ministries: education, health, justice, and interior. Sultan Qaboos also created an Interim Advisory Council, which enacted a development plan to address many of the social issues fueling dissent among Dhofaris.[60]

Under Sultan Qaboos, one month after the coup, Oman joined the Arab League and the United Nations,[61] which signaled the new regime's desire to modernize the country.[62] Britain now had a viable ally in Sultan Qaboos, and quickly developed a plan to assist the Sultan to include the following described by Ladwig: "...the British provided assistance in four key areas: developing a plan for victory; training and expanding the Sultan's Armed Forces; providing experienced leadership and technical skills; and equipping the SAF for counterinsurgency."[63]

Just before the coup, Lieutenant Colonel John Watts, the CO of 22 SAS, took a small team to Oman to make an assessment of the situation in order to determine what could be done to assist the Sultan in defeating the insurgency.[64] Watts' assessment recommended SAS participation along five fronts: intelligence, information, medical support, veterinary support, and "When possible, the raising of Dhofari soldiers to fight for the Sultan."[65] The first SAS team was replaced by a second team led by Tony

Jeapes, at which point the SAS was operating on the first four of the five fronts, but without success on the fifth front of raising Dhofaris to fight for the Sultan.[66]

Many of Sultan Qaboos' reforms addressed the grievances that sparked the insurgency. Arguably the most important reform enacted by Sultan Qaboos was adopting a policy of amnesty. As a result, members of the *adoo* began to surrender to the Sultan's forces, and some acted in support of Sultan Qaboos against the *adoo*. In order to retain support, PFLOAG leadership threatened to execute any *adoo* attempting to surrender. The combination of the Sultan's reforms and the PFLOAG leadership's growing repression came to a head on September 12, 1970 when fighting erupted between PFLOAG hardliners and other *adoo* elements no longer satisfied with the communist agenda.[67]

The heavy-handed tactics and practices of the communists and their forced takeover of the DLF triggered an internal battle in which Salim Mubarak and his core of fighters resisted the communist takeover. Mubarak then led his men off the mountain to surrender to the Sultan's forces.[68] As a result of the internal conflict and the attractive reforms of Sultan Qaboos, Salim Mubarak, the second in command of the Eastern Area of the DLF, and 24[69] of his best fighters defected to the side of the Sultan.[70]

Although a few former insurgent fighters had previously changed sides, they were few and of little influence as most of the insurgents inclined to change sides were skeptical of Sultan Qaboos' promised reforms.[71] Mubarak was the first *adoo* leader of great influence to surrender. Indeed, Mubarak is credited with the idea of forming a *firqa* loyal to the Sultan to not only fight the *adoo*, but also to recruit them to switch sides and support the Sultan.[72]

The arrival of Mubarak and the formation of the *firqa* Saladdin was a turning point in the campaign, but also a learning point. Initial thinking was to mix the tribes within each *firqa* to as a natural check on any one tribe becoming too powerful. After the death of Mubarak, BATT placed Mubarak's second in command as the new leader. [73] Unfortunately, Mubarak's second in command was rejected by the men of the various tribes, and the *firqa* Saladdin collapsed under tribal rivalries and distrust.[74]

While Mubarak's defection was significant, it was only the beginning. In a seven-month period, from September of '70 to March of '71, more than 200 enemy fighters surrendered to the Sultan's forces.[75] In early 1972 there were 11 *firqas* varying in size from 40 to 140 members in each.[76] By the middle of '74 the *firqa* had grown to about 1,000 members,[77] and by the end of the campaign about 20 different *firqas* were formed totaling approximately 3,000 fighters.[78] In the battle for the will of the people, Sultan Qaboos outpaced both his father and the insurgents.

The *firqa* were not only a visible indication of the Sultan's growing support among the population, but also the preferred means of reducing the enemy's ranks. Killing an *adoo* might reduce the enemy by one, but might also create a tribal blood feud that could add to the conflict. If, however, the Sultan's forces could convince an *adoo* to surrender and join the Sultan's *firqa,* the gain would be a "plus two" as the *adoo* lose one, and the Sultan gains one.[79] A former SAF officer Ian Gardiner describes the mindset of the former *adoo* joining the *firqas*:

> The *Firqat* Forces units were made up of Dhofari Jebeli tribesmen, many of whom had been fighting on the other side but who had been persuaded to come over to the Sultan. These people were called Surrendered Enemy Personnel - SEPs - but it was a misnomer because it implied that they had been beaten. As soldiers, they were not beaten, but the political system which had recruited them was.[80]

By the end of 1970, the situation in Oman had changed dramatically. Sultan Qaboos deposed his father and instituted long overdue reforms to include amnesty. Sultan Qaboos pushed for Omanis to join the SAF while Britain sent SAS to serve as British Advisory Training Teams (BATTs) to assist the Sultan. The BATTs began training the first *firqa,* Saladdin, at Mirbat. Sultan Qaboos ordered the formation of the Dhofar Brigade[81] in 1970 to provide a permanent presence in Dhofar as opposed to the constant rotation of forces in and out of Dhofar under his father's reign.[82] Headquartered at RAF Salalah, the Dhofar Brigade encompassed all of the Sultan's forces in Dhofar regardless of service.[83]

With so many changes occurring in such a short period of time it is difficult to determine the level of impact of any one change. Many veterans of the campaign credit the *firqas* as being critical to the success of the campaign. As Ian Gardiner put it, "For all their limitations, I do not believe we could have won the war without the *Firqat*."[84] Similarly, John Akehurst described the role of the *firqa,* "I must reiterate how vitally important the *Firqats* were in the struggle. Their knowledge of the ground and their influence with the civilians were indispensible, and worth all the time, trouble and money spent to secure and retain their goodwill and allegiance."[85]

1971

Over the next year, BATT continued to develop *firqas* as the Sultan's reforms continued to attract additional *adoo* surrenders. By assisting the Sultan in raising, training, and employing the surrendered enemy personnel as *firqa,* the SAS/BATT were acting along Watts' fifth front, raising Dhofaris to fight for the Sultan. Operation JAGUAR began in 1971 with the aim of reestablishing a foothold on the *jebel.* Operation JAGUAR involved two SAS Squadrons (B and G), and three newly raised *firqas.* The end result of the operation was the establishment of a foothold on the *jebel* from which the Sultan's forces could patrol, signaling the determination to remain permanently. From the foothold established during Operation Jaguar, SAF, SAS, and *firqa* began moving slowly but steadily westward across the *jebel* to clear away the *adoo* and establish the Sultan's control in Dhofar.[86]

From the beginning of 1971 with Operation JAGUAR, the general strategy was to clear an area of *adoo*, establish *firqa* to hold their tribal areas once cleared, and continuously push the *adoo* west. The enemy was strongest in the Western Area of Dhofar and as such, SAF would require a large force to deal with them in the difficult terrain of the *jebel*. To this end, the decision was made to employ the *firqa* to hold the Eastern and Central Areas once cleared to allow regular SAF and allied[87] units to mass in the west.[88]

The use of the *firqa* to hold cleared areas was a slight change in the original vision for the irregular force. The original concept was to raise a small force of specially selected[89] recruits numbering no more than 100 to conduct ambushes, interdiction of enemy supply routes, pre-planned raids, raising and leading their tribes against the *adoo*, and to conduct diversionary actions in support of SAF operations.[90] As the numbers of *adoo* changing sides to fight for the Sultan grew, the plan was modified to allow for a maximum of 700 total fighters.[91] Eventually this figure was thrown out as well as the Sultan ended the campaign with about 3,000 fighters in his *firqas*.

While there was motivation to accept all comers into the *firqa* as a means of keeping the Dhofaris on side,[92] there were some screening criteria. As recorded in BATT Notes on the Raising and Training of Irregular Forces in Dhofar, "The most important factor in selecting an irregular indigenous force is to establish their true motive for fighting and to use this as a bait as much as possible. In this way a force will be created using its own motivation which will hold it together and keep it going in difficult times."[93]

Other criteria used in Dhofar include age and overall health. Recruits that were too old, too young, or in very sick were rejected as unfit for the rigors of combat.[94]

While Operation JAGUAR had some success in establishing permanent SAF and *firqa* bases in the Central Area, it failed to achieve its original aim which was to clear the Eastern Area of enemy. Retention of the base areas on the *jebel* did signal a renewed strength and resolve on the part of the Sultan's forces, and enabled patrolling in the area by SAF and *firqa* forces. Previous attempts to establish a permanent base on the *jebel* met with failure and eventual withdrawal. Operation JAGUAR was different and the base established at Medinat Al Haq, known as "White City" to the SAS, remained throughout the campaign.[95]

1972

In 1972 PFLOAG attacked from inside Yemen across the border to seize the town of Habarut just inside the Omani border. The Sultan responded by sending his air force to attack the Yemeni town of Hauf a few weeks later. PFLOAG's next move was an attack on the outpost at Mirbat on 19 July.[96] Mirbat defenders, 30 men altogether, included local town guards, *firqa*, an eight man BATT from B Squadron, Dhofar Gendarmerie, and a 25-pound field gun.[97] PFLOAG massed more than 200 fighters to attack the outpost.[98]

The PFLOAG force made one critical mistake in that they opened fire with indirect weapons too soon that alerted the assembled defenders of the attack before the ground troops could press home the assault.[99] Additionally, G Squadron was armed and on their way to conduct ranges when the attack went in and were able to quickly conduct a counter-attack against the PFLOAG fighters. The BATT also made good use of Strikemaster attack aircraft from the Sultan of Oman's Air Force in breaking up the PFLOAG assault.[100]

PFLOAG lost 30 percent of its attacking force as killed in action during the assault on Mirbat, and never tried such a large scale direct assault again.[101] Instead, in order to relieve pressure on PFLOAG forces in Dhofar, PFLOAG tried to renew their attacks in Northern Oman. As described previously, the plot was uncovered and thwarted.

Also in 1972, as SAF pressure increased, the PFLOAG attempted another coordinated attack in the north to cause SAF to draw resources northward, thus relieving some of the pressure in the Center Area and Eastern Area (PFLOAG had divided Dhofar into three areas, Western, Center, and Eastern).[102] Arms were smuggled, recruiting increased, and a plan was formed. *Adoo* misfortune again, the SAF uncovered the plot and thwarted the plan. This led to the capture of the *adoo* leaders as well as other collaborators. In the end, 77 people involved in the plot were convicted and sentenced either to life in prison or death by firing squad.[103]

Other operations in 1972 built upon the gains of Operation JAGUAR, and included Operations HORNBEAM, SYCAMORE, and HAWK. The aim of these operations was to interdict enemy supplies going to the Eastern Area to support destruction of the enemy operating there. As with Operation JAGUAR, these operations failed to eliminate the enemy in the Eastern Area but did result in the capture of 80 fighters and smuggled arms as well as an overall disruptive effect on PFLOAG.[104]

1973

The long-term impact of Operation JAGUAR and the permanent bases on the *jebel* became more evident in 1973. Operating from these bases throughout the monsoon, SAF, *firqa*, and allied forces made significant strides towards controlling the Eastern Area. These gains include the opening of the Midway Road by the Iranian contingent, the beginning and completion of the Hornbeam Line, as well as the civil aid activities by the Royal Engineers on the *jebel*. In addition to the permanent bases on the *jebel*, deployment of an Abu Dhabi Defence Force battalion to Northern Oman to relieve SAF forces operating there enabled SAF to increase the number of troops operating in Dhofar.[105]

The Midway Road was a vital line of communication because it was the only link between Salalah and Northern Oman overland. Until the Iranian forces reopened the Midway Road in 1973, all movement between Northern Oman and Salalah had to be conducted by air.[106] With limited air transport assets, control of the Midway Road greatly improved the mobility and sustainability of the Sultan's forces in Dhofar.

The Hornbeam Line was the first major obstacle emplaced to disrupt *adoo* movement from the Western Area eastward. The line consisted of wire and mines and included base areas at regular intervals to enable patrolling. While the line did not prevent enemy personnel from crossing, the crossing points where the line was breached were easy to identify. The Sultan's forces would follow up crossings with air reconnaissance and/or ground trackers to locate the intruders. The Hornbeam Line did prevent the *adoo* from transporting large quantities of materiel as it could not be crossed by camels or other pack animals.[107]

Civil aid on the *jebel* was given top priority among civil aid projects by Sultan Qaboos.[108] This was part of the Sultan's priorities for the fighting season of '72-'73 which also included securing the Oman-Yemen border and defending the Salalah plain.[109] Newly formed Civil Action Teams augmented the civil aid efforts by coordinating aid efforts such as drilling wells, building schools, and medical assistance visits in an effort to establish governance and address the local grievances fueling the insurgency.[110]

All of these efforts, the Hornbeam Line, opening the Midway Road, increasing civil aid, were components of Sultan Qaboos' plan, but were coordinated under the Commander of the Sultan's Armed Forces (CSAF) at the time, Major General Timothy Creasy. Creasy took Sultan's Qaboos' priorities and developed a plan to achieve them, which focused on interdicting the movement of *adoo* from west to the Eastern Area in order to clear the Eastern Area.[111] While PFLOAG had previously divided Dhofar into Western, Central, and Eastern Areas for coordination purposes, the Sultan's forces under CSAF Creasy were physically dividing Dhofar to impede *adoo* freedom of maneuver, interdict *adoo* logistics, and systematically clear the *adoo* from east to west.

1974

In 1974 CSAF Creasy directed the Dhofar Brigade, which was then commanded by Brigadier John Akehurst, to clear the Eastern Area and continue to push west.[112] The Dhofar Brigade in 1974 was approximately 10,000 strong and included Omani forces, and foreign forces from Britain, Iran, and Jordan.[113] The Dhofar Brigade included four infantry battalions, two Omani and two Baluch.[114] The brigade also included the Oman Artillery Regiment which had a variety of guns from 5.5-inch medium guns to 4.2-inch mortars, an Armoured Car Squadron (half of which remained in Northern Oman) equipped with forty-eight armored cars mounting 76mm guns, and a mobile patrol unit called Z Company mounted in Land Rovers carrying .50-caliber machine guns.[115] Last but not least, in 1974 the Dhofar Brigade had about 1,000 fighters in its *firqas* with more joining every week.[116]

In order to carry out his instructions from CSAF Creasy, Brigadier Akehurst created his battle plan:

> The *Firqats* at that time were about 1,400 strong and were the key to the centre and east. Considerable strength would be needed to take on the enemy in the west and it could only be amassed at the expense of the centre and east. Either the enemy must be cleaned out altogether, an impossible task in the short term, or the securing must be taken over by the *Firqats*. If roads could be built to those places now supplied by air, especially helicopters, more resources still would be made available for the west.[117]

Firqas had grown since Mubarak led his band down from the mountain, and had certainly contributed to the Sultan's campaign. Beginning in 1974, the *firqa* would play a larger role in the defeat of the *adoo*.

Brigadier Akehurst, building on the successes of the previous years (e.g. regaining control of the Midway Road, completion of the Hornbeam Line, permanent bases on the *jebel*), combined the military capabilities at his disposal (e.g. Omani battalions, Iranian forces, supporting arms), the civil aid resources (e.g. the Civil Aid Department, Civil Action Teams), and the *firqa* to clear the Eastern Area of *adoo*, hold it to prevent *adoo* return, and improve the civil infrastructure to consolidate support for the Sultan. The *firqa* played a key role in the execution of Akehurst's plan:

> The Jebali people were intensely tribal and very jealous of their own tribe's lands and customs … Several *Firqats* were formed from surrendered enemy but had to live on the Salalah Plain or in other secure areas not their own because the enemy prevented occupation of their tribal areas. From conversations with their leaders and their SAS advisers I learned of their intense desire to reoccupy their own land. All of them promised instant security if they could be established in positions of their own choosing. . . If good and constant water could be provided at a central point, most civilians could be expected to come

into that point and there be persuaded that the Government was offering the better deal.[118]

Akehurst saw a way to use the *firqas* natural motivation to return to and secure their tribal areas to support his campaign. He describes the first step in his 10-point pattern as "A SAF operation in strength supported by a *Firqat* secures a position of the *Firqat's* choice which dominated its tribal area."[119]

The first operation to establish *firqas* in their tribal areas on the *jebel* took place in October of 1974[120] and involved the *firqa* Abu Bakar Sadeeq establishing a position at Jebel Kaftawt.[121] To further support disruption of enemy movement east on the *jebel*, SAF constructed a supplementary line called the Hammer Line which ran for about five kilometers near Jebel Kaftawt. In addition to the establishment of *firqa* Abu Bakar Sadeeq, additional *firqa* established positions at Hagleet, Zeak, Ashinhaib, Ayun, and Burg Haluf.[122]

Although the positive benefits of placing *firqa* in their tribal areas began to show in less than a month (e.g. increased surrenders, vital intelligence on the enemy situation),[123] the Sultan was unsure what to do with the *firqa* once the war ended.[124] Some advocated for the *firqa* to be developed and organized into a National Guard, but this plan was rejected for two main reasons. First, the tribesmen of the *jebel* were not accustomed to discipline and training, and would likely spend a good deal of time absent. Second, the Sultan did not trust the *firqa* completely as they were recently fighting against him.[125] Providing them better weapons, training, and organization was too great a risk to take. In the end, the Sultan determined to keep the *firqa* as tribal forces which would secure their own areas with small arms.[126]

A third and final attempt to open a new front in Northern Oman involved a member of PFLOAG's central committee from Beirut who was killed at a checkpoint by a SAF soldier on 29 October 1974. In the committee member's vehicle were money, weapons, explosives, and evidence of planned attacks. Due to rapid exploitation of the information found in the vehicle, Omani security forces were able to make additional arrests and foil the plot.[127]

1975

The next major operation in the Dhofar campaign involved an assault to destroy the very large *adoo* arms cache in the Sherishitti cave complex west of the Damavand Line. Beginning in January 1975, Operation Dharab originally called for the Iranian contingent to seize the Sherishitti caves, but CSAF later gave the task to the Dhofar Brigade commanded by Akehurst.[128] The plan called for a SAF battalion supported by 40 men from the Tariq Bin Zeead and Southern Mahra *firqas* along with their BATTs.[129]

Apparently forgetting the lesson of the first *firqa* Saladdin which disintegrated under tribal friction,[130] a mixed *firqa* was formed to lead the SAF companies into their planned positions for the assault on the caves at Sherishitti. The mixed *firqa* had no cohesion, and thus no confidence, especially as the lead element against what was believed to be a very hard target.[131] Bryan Ray describes the effect of the mixed *firqa* during Operation DHARAB. "Disastrously, however, surprise for the operation was lost because of the heavy supporting fire insisted on by the *firqas* before moving forward. Thus alerted, the *adoo* were ready and waiting in excellent ambush positions which dominated the line of the SAF advance."[132] Operation DHARAB, although not well executed, eventually achieved the overall aim of removing the Sherishitti caves as an *adoo* supply depot.

The next major operation, called Operation HIMAAR, would mark one of the last operations conducted to gain control of the Central and Eastern Areas. SAF operations between the Hornbeam and Damavand Lines, such as Operation HIMAAR, resulted in the destruction of the 9th June Regiment of the *adoo*,[133] and left only the Western Area to clear of *adoo*. The Sultan would gain control over all Dhofar at the conclusion of the next and final major operation, Operation HADAF.

The overall aim of Operation HADAF was to establish a new defensive line to continue to increase pressure on the Western Area while remaining out of range of indirect fire originating from Yemen. Operation HADAF included deception operations to confuse and disintegrate the *adoo* operating in the objective area. The deceptions included tactical movements, false communications, and other means intended to convince the *adoo* that the objectives of the pending operation were the coastal pass below the Sarfait position and the Sherishitti cave complex.[134]

The *adoo* were not fooled by the deception involving Sarfait as they believed any operations there were for deception only, and not sustainable. Because of the *adoo* lack of reaction and the resultant success at Sarfait, as well as the adamant insistence of the *firqa*[135] involved to hold onto the ground gained, Akehurst requested CSAF support a change in the operation.[136] The new CSAF, Major General Ken Perkins, agreed and approved the change.[137]

The final major operation would sweep the remaining *adoo* and Yemeni troops from the Western Area. The success of the operation not only placed all of Dhofar under the Sultan's control, but also resulted in 222 surrenders between mid-October and the end of the year 1975.[138] Akehurst sent Sultan Qaboos a message on behalf of CSAF, "I have the honour to inform your Majesty that Dhofar is now secure for civil development."[139] Sultan Qaboos announced the end of the war on 11 December 1975.[140]

Conclusions

The role of the *firqa* in the campaign was vital, but is often overblown.

The *firqa* filled a gap in capability that SAF could never fill. The *firqa* were Dhofaris and Jebalis who knew the land and had the trust of the people. By the same token, the *firqa* alone could never have achieved success against PFLOAG. The interdependence of the forces involved in the campaign was illustrated by Jeapes:

> The *firqats'* understanding of ground and their speed of manoeuvre were both superior to SAF troops', but when it came to straight military tactics, the SAF's discipline told every time. The two forces were complementary; neither could have won the war alone. If the *firqats* were the most important Government department to be created to win the war, Civil Aid must run them a close second. The Civil Aid department was, I believe, the one new lesson the Dhofar Campaign provided in the study of counter-revolutionary war, yet it came about almost by default.[141]

SAF and BATT both recognized the *firqa* as critical to success, but had different views of the purpose of these irregular forces. While generically the Watts Plan called for recruiting indigenous forces to the side of the Sultan – "When possible, the raising of Dhofari soldiers to fight for the Sultan"[142] – this does not truly capture the purpose of the *firqa*. General Sir Peter De La Billiere, who served in multiple campaigns from the Korean War to the Gulf War of 1991 to include campaigns in Malaya, Aden, Borneo, and Dhofar offered his insights:

> As in Malaya and Borneo, our aim was to help local people help themselves. ... From the beginning the key element in our plans were the *firqats* ... we began to recruit and train irregular soldiers loyal to the Sultan. .... Our aim was that they should defend the settlements on the plain, and also lure rebels down off the *jebel*. ... Only by training native soldiers could we build up a force large enough to defeat the rebels. . . [143]

According to Sir Peter, the purpose of the *firqa* was to increase the strength of the Sultan's forces by holding cleared areas and enticing their fellow tribesmen to quit the *adoo* and join with the Sultan. To achieve a victory that would last, the peoples of Oman had to help themselves.[144]

Continuing in this vein, Major General Tony Jeapes offered his philosophy on recruiting irregular security forces from the ranks of the enemy:

> Persuading a man to join you is far cheaper than killing him. Words are far, far less expensive than bullets, let alone shells and bombs. Then, too, by killing him you merely deprive the enemy of one soldier. If he is persuaded to join the Government forces the enemy again becomes one less, but the Government forces become one more, a gain of plus two.[145]

Jeapes saw the role of the *firqa* as gaining a victory over the insurgents by winning over their membership through persuasion and example while reducing the level of violence. Jeapes saw increased defections to the side of the Sultan as a psychological blow to the *adoo*. Jeapes related an account which demonstrated the impact of *firqa* on the psyche of the *adoo*:

> One thinks again of the political commissar of the *adoo firqat* defending Shershitti who surrendered during Operation Badree. … If ever a man was a Communist, it was surely he, but when asked why he had come across to the Government he replied, "Because you are here – and you could not be here in the West unless the loyal *firqats* were with you. You would not have any *firqats* unless the people supported them you would only have that support if the rumours of progress and development I have heard are true. If they are true, then the Front has told me lies. If they lied on that, they have probably lied on other things. Therefore I have surrendered to you."[146]

As Akehurst mentioned in his book, by assuming a local security role in less-contested areas in the east, the *firqa* created the opportunity for SAF to concentrate more forces for offensive operations as early as 1971.[147] As the commander of the Dhofar Brigade, Akehurst was more focused on the *firqa* as increased manpower which would enable him to focus his conventional forces on the conventional fight. Akehurst recognized the strengths and the weaknesses of the *firqa* and incorporated them into his plan accordingly.[148]

Both the SAF and BATT views of the purpose of the *firqa* were complementary. It is important to note as well that the *firqa* themselves understood and accepted their role, and had a voice in shaping operations and how they were employed.[149] The overriding aim of the *firqa* was to regain control over their tribal lands.[150]

The combined purposes of the *firqa* (e.g. SAF, BATT, *firqa*) fit into, and indeed helped shape the Sultan's strategy over time. Watt's five-point plan constituted more of an assessment and identification of lines of operation than an actual strategy.[151] Although Watts is credited with the idea of raising indigenous forces to fight for the Sultan,[152] the plan did not reach any level of detail or result in any concrete steps toward forming an indigenous force prior to the defection of Salim Mubarak and his followers.[153] The surrender of Salim Mubarak was not only unexpected, but also caught the Sultan's forces without a plan to deal with surrendered enemy personnel. As one SAS veteran of Dhofar related the surrender of Mubarak, "First of all the surrender of Mubarak took us all by surprise. Nobody knew he was coming in. He was a *firqa* leader with the *adoo*, so his position was known . . . His actual arrival surprised everybody. Nobody knew what to do with him or where to put him."[154] Despite the slow start, once BATT and others recognized the potential of forming *firqa* from surrendered enemy personnel, recruiting *adoo* became a key part of the campaign and operations.[155]

Because the *adoo* outnumbered the SAF, and in many cases had better equipment, reversing the gains of PFLOAG in Dhofar required greater combat power to clear the *adoo* from the *jebel*. Increased combat power came after Sultan Qaboos authorized increases in his conventional forces, and the *firqa* assumed the local security role in their tribal lands in the Eastern Area,[156] thus releasing SAF forces for offensive operations.[157] As SAF regained footholds on the *jebel* and slowly pushed west, BATT and *firqa* supported SAF operations by conducting reconnaissance and security operations ahead of SAF, and communicated with the local population to gain support for the Sultan and to recruit *adoo* to join the *firqa*.[158]

In addition to increasing the combat power of the Sultan, formation of *firqa* from surrendered enemies greatly reduced the combat power available to PFLOAG. McKeown's research estimates the PFLOAG strength at the end of 1969 as 2,000 organized fighters and 3,000 militia fighters which constituted nearly the entire population of the *jebel*.[159] Assuming the population of the *jebel* remained fairly constant, this gave the PFLOAG approximately 5,000 fighters. By the end of March 1971, more than 200 *adoo* surrendered to the Sultan's forces,[160] which would put PFLOAG strength at about 4,800. This shift in combat power continued and by the end of the campaign, with approximately 3,000 fighters in the Sultan's *firqas*,[161] PFLOAG strength would have been approximately 2,000. This constituted a significant shift in combat power directly from one side to the other, and demonstrated the effectiveness of the strategy.

Although the *firqa* in this campaign did not exist until 1970, they played a vital role in the successful outcome. Those involved in the campaign provided several insights into raising, training, and employing the Dhofari irregular security forces known as *firqa*, or as Tony Jeapes humorously put it, "...the SAS did not always talk of the *firqats*, they called them the firkins or the firks or even, in moments of stress, both."[162] The composition of the *firqa* was based on tribal affiliation and the number of fighters available. For example, in 1972 there were 11 *firqas* which varied in size from 40 to 140 fighters.[163] *Firqas* were armed with small arms, but did not receive heavy machine guns or mortars.[164] Each *firqa* had at a minimum a four-man BATT assigned to it which conducted training, joined the *firqa* on operations,[165] and served as the link between the *firqa* and SAF.

Indeed, without BATT the success of the *firqa* may have been out of reach due to the unique requirements for effective *firqa* advisers. As Ian Gardiner pointed out, SAS soldiers were better suited than most to working with the *firqa*. "Regular soldiers could find the *Firqat* infuriating. The SAS, who themselves were somewhat irregular, and were trained to train irregular soldiers, were mostly pretty well adjusted to the task."[166] In one of many compliments to the SAS who worked with the *firqa*, Akehurst concluded, "BATT's contribution in raising and training the *Firqats* had been of inestimable importance in the winning of the war . . ."[167]

The *firqa* members elected their leaders, one military and one political.[168] BATT commanders would coordinate with the *firqa* leaders, but the BATT commanders were also in command of the *firqa* itself.[169] While BATT served as effective advisers and commanders of the Sultan's *firqa*, they also learned from the *firqa* fighters[170] and adapted their tactics accordingly.

The *firqa* were uniquely familiar with the capabilities and tactics of their enemies as they previously defected from the ranks of the enemy to join the Sultan. The key enemy advantages in the Dhofar campaign were legitimate grievances with Sultan Said which they could exploit to gain support of the population, numerical superiority over SAF, and superior equipment. Once Sultan Qaboos seized power and enacted reforms, the enemy advantage of the support of the population was contested, and finally lost to the Sultan.[171]

As mentioned above, the PFLOAG had approximately 5,000 fighters on the *jebel* at its high water mark at the end of 1969. Defections to the Government side were costly in terms of manpower, but possibly more costly psychologically. As fighters left the *adoo* to join the Sultan's *firqa*, they brought with them and shared their knowledge of enemy tactics and tricks, one instance of which was described by a former SAS Dhofar veteran:

> What he said they used to do was come in quite close under the cover of darkness, they would put down a volley of fully automatic fire at about ten feet, and they would send what they called their commandos in under the tracer and used to find the Iranians all cowering in their sangars. And they just used to put their AK-47s over the top of the sangars and they just used to spray them. On that particular night they tried it with us, and fortunately we were ready for them and they lost casualties that night rather than ourselves. We had a couple of lightly wounded. That process of how the *adoo* used to do with the Iranians was explained to me by one of our surrendered enemy personnel.[172]

Due to support from Communist China and the Soviet Union,[173] PFLOAG was well equipped, often having better small arms and mortars than SAF.[174] As the Sultan committed additional resources to modernizing his forces, the enemy advantages in small arms diminished. As most *firqa* operated with BATT support,[175] the SAF were usually able to overmatch enemy firepower with SAF artillery or attack aviation support.[176]

PFLOAG also benefited from training support, with a select few receiving training in China[177] consisting of six months of training on political and military topics.[178] Jeapes described an operation to capture of the coastal town of Sudh in February 1971. During this operation, Salim Mubarak used his Communist-supplied training to great effect. After a daring nighttime landing from the sea, the *Firqa* Saladdin and their BATT took control of the city without violence. After raising the Omani flag over the fort in the center of the town, the *firqa* leader Salim Mubarak shouted to the city that the *firqa* were here to stay, the communists were defeated, and that all of the men should assemble at 10:00 a.m. that morning. Once all of the men were gathered from their homes, Mubarak put his training under the communists to good work.[179] As Jeapes recounted in his book *SAS Secret War*, "I realized that what I had witnessed was a Communist takeover in reverse. Salim had used the methods he had been taught in China. It was a perfectly executed example of indoctrination such as no SAF or British troops could possibly have achieved."[180]

The campaign in Dhofar against the DLF and PFLOAG was a success. Many factors contributed to the successful outcome. Sultan Qaboos was an enlightened ruler who understood the grievances of his people and was willing to make concessions to alleviate their grievances. The Communists supporting the PFLOAG pushed the Dhofaris too far in their assault on tribalism and Islam.[181] Sultan Qaboos pursued a policy of amnesty which was accepted by many whose previous reasons for fighting had been removed by Sultan Qaboos' other reforms. Iran and Jordan agreed to support Sultan Qaboos in his fight and provided resources vital to the overall success of the campaign.

The success of Sultan Qaboos was not a foregone conclusion upon his assumption of power. From 1965 to 1970, Sultan Said lost most of Dhofar to DLF and PFLOAG, failed to increase his security force's capabilities, and continued to alienate the people of Dhofar and the *Jebel*. Despite the constant presence of security forces in Northern Oman, Sultan Said's enemies were emboldened enough by his weakness to attack outposts in Northern Oman as training operations.

Sultan Qaboos did not win through superior forces – he was outnumbered and outgunned in 1970. He did not win because he raised irregular security forces – there were none when he took power. Sultan Qaboos did not prevail due to overwhelming external support – the SAS "were never there," only a small number of British Army Training Teams and seconded and contracted officers. Sultan Qaboos won because he was willing and able to regain the support of the people through a combination of reforms to address legitimate grievances, security operations to remove enemy forces and secure his people, and civil aid projects to demonstrate his resolve and concern for the well-being of his people.

Notes

1.   Ian Beckett, "The British Counter-insurgency Campaign in Dhofar, 1965-1975," *Counterinsurgency in Modern Warfare*, Daniel Marston and Carter Malkasian, (eds) (Oxford: Osprey Publishing, 2010), 175. "Indeed, it has often been described as a model counterinsurgency campaign, displaying both the fruits of the operational experience gained by the British Army since 1945, and also the flexible British approach to such things."

2.   Lieutenant Colonel John McKeown, *Britain and Oman: The Dhofar War and Its Significance*, (Cambridge, UK: Dissertation submitted for the degree of Master of Philosophy in the University of Cambridge, 1981), 96.

3.   John Akehurst, *We Won a War: The Campaign in Oman 1965-1975*. (Great Britain: Biddles Ltd., 1982), 183. "I think the Sultan's success came mainly from four mistakes by the enemy and six things that he and his Armed Forces got right.":

> *Enemy Mistakes*
> 1. Trying to replace the simple but deep Islamic faith of the Jebalis with Communist atheism.
> 2. Trying to break down tribalism before the people were ready for it.
> 3. A cumbersome command and communications structure.
> 4. Reliance on a single supply line.
>
> *Features of the Sultan's Success*
> 1. The coup and the reforms which followed it.
> 2. Concentrating attention on winning the support of the population away from the enemy.
> 3. Joint civil/military control.
> 4. Interrupting the enemy's supply line.
> 5. Air power, especially helicopters.
> 6. Intelligence.

4.   Ian Gardiner, *In the Service of the Sultan: A First Hand Account of the Dhofar Insurgency*. (South Yorkshire, England: Pen & Sword Books Unlimited, 2007), 156.

5.   D.L. Price, *Oman: Insurgency and Development*, (London: Institute for the Study of Conflict, 1975), 1.

6.   Beckett, "The British Counter-insurgency Campaign in Dhofar," 175.

7.   Bard O'Neill, "Revolutionary War in Oman," *Insurgency in the Modern World*, (Boulder, Colorado: Westview Press, 1980), 213.

8.   Beckett, "The British Counter-insurgency Campaign in Dhofar," 175.

9.   Cited from notes taken during a lecture by Dr. Daniel Marston on 18 January 2011.

10. Marston lecture, 18 January 2011.

11. Walter Ladwig III, *Supporting Allies in COIN: Britain and the Dhofar Rebellion, Small Wars and Insurgencies*, Vol. 19:1 March 2008, p. 66.

12. Ladwig, *Supporting Allies in COIN*, 64.

13. McKeown, *Britain and Oman*, 17-18. "Sultan Said bin Sultan despatched a force from Muscat to annex the province but the force was soon withdrawn. A second annexation took place in 1879 at the invitation of a leader of a revolution against a Moplah priest who had fled India and established personal leadership in Salalah. From 1879, Dhofar remained continuously under the Sultan's rule through his appointed wali. Rebellions were frequent. In 1880 and 1883, there were risings which the small local garrison could contain. In 1885 and 1887, more serious rebellions needed forces from Muscat to restore the situation. The most serious rebellion, in 1895, was ended only when British assistance was accepted and an Anglo-Omani force sent by sea in 1897. There were minor uprisings until 1900, when the end of foreign intrigue by the displaced Moplah in Constantinople, and the permanent transfer of the unpopular wali 'whose proceedings were generally characterized by energy rather than discretion,' led to peace."

14. Ladwig, *Supporting Allies in COIN*, 64.

15. General Sir Peter De La Billiere, *Looking for Trouble: SAS to Gulf Command, The Autobiography*, (London: Harper Collins, 1995), 132. "Three rebel leaders — Sheikh Ghalib bin Ali, his younger brother Talib bin Ali, and Sheikh Suleiman bin Himayer — had established themselves on top of the Jebel Akhdar — literally Green Mountain — a massif with a flat top 8000 feet above sea level, and all efforts to evict them had been in vain. The prime mover of the revolt appeared to be Ghalib, an imam, or religious leader, who had defied the Sultan; but Talib had had military experience, and was thought to be in command of the dissident army. Suleiman was Paramount Sheikh of the Bani Riyam, the principal mountain tribe. All three were being financed and armed by Saudi Arabia, who had sent them arms, mines, and gold." See also Sir Frank Kitson's account of this campaign in his book, *Bunch of Five,* (London: Faber and Faber 1977).

16. British Army Tactical Retrieval Cell, Notes from Dhofar presentations, (Alanbrooke Hall, Staff College, UK, 30 June 1982), 4.

17. Akehurst, *We Won a War*, 31. "SAF was born of an exchange of letters in 1958 between Julian Amery, then Parliamentary Under-Secretary of State at the Foreign Office in the British Conservative Government, and Sultan Said bin Taimur. It was one of the moves that in 1959 enabled the Sultan, with substantial British help, quickly to put down a rebellion in the Jebel Akhdar. For the next ten years British officers and NCOs continued to be seconded to SAF, but money, arms and equipment — even uniforms — remained in short supply. Soldiers, especially those who drove or maintained vehicles, became masters of improvisation."

18. For a more detailed discussion of the campaign, see General Sir Peter De La Billiere, *Looking for Trouble: SAS to Gulf Command, The Autobiography*, London, Harper Collins, 1995, chapter nine.

19. Beckett, "The British Counter-insurgency Campaign in Dhofar," 176.

20. BL330, SAS Dhofar veteran, interview by Robert Green, 28 March 2011. "My understanding, and this is from talking to members of the firqa, and talking to some of the more senior people in Salalah, it was felt that he, as I said the main aim of the Sultan was to keep the Dhofari unspoiled, and keep the worst aspects of civilization out of Dhofar basically."

21. Beckett, "The British Counter-insurgency Campaign in Dhofar," 179.

22. Paul Sibley, *A Monk in the SAS*, (London: Spiderwise Publishing, 2011), 299.

23. Beckett, "The British Counter-insurgency Campaign in Dhofar," 176.

24. Akehurst, *We Won a War*, 13. "Until 1967 Said could plead poverty to support his denial of development, but then oil revenues began and despite a declaration of intent no development occurred. He claimed that he must wait until the cash built up before taking any action. Investment was the same as borrowing; borrowing meant usury; and usury was expressly forbidden by the Koran. He held an unshakable belief in a cash economy and eventually suffered the fate of Canute as the tide of progress rolled in."

25. Beckett, "The British Counter-insurgency Campaign in Dhofar," 176. "The insurgency was primarily a result of the feudal and increasingly authoritarian style of Sultan Said bin Taimur, who had ruled Oman since 1932. No one was allowed to leave the country (nor, indeed, to move from one area to another) without permission, and this was rarely granted. There were only three state-run schools in the whole of Oman, their exclusively male pupils chosen by the sultan and denied education beyond primary level. The only hospital was run, under sufferance, by an American mission, and diseases such as malaria, trachoma, and glaucoma were endemic. All symbols of modernity were banned, from medical drugs to spectacles, radios, bicycles, cigarettes, trousers, music, and dancing. … Matters were exacerbated by the failure to use any of the growing oil revenues for the benefit of the Omani people."

26. Price, *Oman: Insurgency and Development*, 3-4. Referring to the Dhofar Charitable Association, "Its politics were mixed — nationalist, Marxist, Nasserite — but primarily it was opposed to the Sultan's rule and to the British connection. Its purpose was, ostensibly, to build mosques and aid the poor; in reality it collected funds, recruited members and established political contacts for the purpose of armed rebellion against the Al Bu Said dynasty and British influence in the region."

27. Sibley, *A Monk in the SAS*, 293.

28. This was a loose organization of Dhofari members of police or military forces of the various Gulf States.

29. Sibley, *A Monk in the SAS*, 293-294.

30. McKeown, *Britain and Oman*, 33. "At the end of 1966, Colonel Lewis considered there was military stalemate. Because of manpower and equipment shortages SAF was unable to destroy the rebel movement, though it was in a poor moral and physical state. He recommended increased military measures such as collective punishments against tribes and evacuation of free-fire zones. He also pressed for political moves."

31. McKeown, *Britain and Oman*, 33.

32. McKeown, *Britain and Oman*, 34. Citing a 1981 interview with a source who was a senior intelligence officer during the time in question, " 'We were talking to people on the jebel, particularly the sheikhs,' recalled the senior intelligence officer at the time. 'They said if His Highness would give some reasonable terms they could pull most people out of the conflict.'"

33. Beckett, "The British Counter-insurgency Campaign in Dhofar," 178.

34. McKeown, *Britain and Oman*, 40. "In August, the change from tribal rebellion to Communist revolution culminated at a congress in the Wadi Hamrin. The newly elected 25-man General Command included only three of the original 18-man DLF executive. The Front was renamed the Popular Front for the Liberation of the Occupied Arabian Gulf (PFLOAG), with the aim of spreading armed struggle throughout the Gulf."

35. Sibley, *A Monk in the SAS*, 297.

36. McKeown, *Britain and Oman*, 40. "The ideology was officially changed from nationalism to Marxism-Leninism and the revolutionary transformation of Dhofar planned."

37. Beckett, "The British Counter-insurgency Campaign in Dhofar," 178.

38. Beckett, "The British Counter-insurgency Campaign in Dhofar," 178. "In the course of 1968, indeed, contacts between the SAF and the insurgents increased from one to two per week, to two to three per day. In the end, SAF was compelled to withdraw from western Dhofar, leaving rebel supply lines untouched and the jebalis unprotected."

39. Beckett, "The British Counter-insurgency Campaign in Dhofar," 177. "The sultan's response to the DLF proved weak and ineffective, the SAF comprising only two British-officered battalions ... neither battalion was stationed in Dhofar, nor were they recruited from Oman; most came from Baluchistan, a province once ruled by Oman. ... A third battalion was raised in 1966 as the Desert Regiment. Initial operations were made difficult by the unfamiliarity of SAF personnel with the area and its inhabitants."

40. Andrew F. Krepinevich, Jr., *The Army and Vietnam*, The John Hopkins University Press, 1986, p. 13.

41. James Corum, Training Indigenous Forces in Counterinsurgency: A Tale of Two Insurgents. http: www.strategicstudiesinstitute.army.mil/pubs/display cfm?PubID=648 (accessed 13 March 2011): 11.

42. Angel Rabasa, Lesley Anne Warner, Peter Chalk, Ivan Khilko, Paraag Shukla, "Money in the Bank Lessons Learned from Past Counterinsurgency (COIN) Operations," National Defense Research Institute, RAND Corporation, 2007, p. 72. "The use of indigenous forces, especially forces from the particular area in question, increases the legitimacy of the counterinsurgents and can also help to divide and weaken the insurgency by psychologically unhinging the insurgents."

43. Rabasa, et al, *Money in the Bank*, p. 74. "In recruiting indigenous security forces, the counterinsurgents should seek to create a force that reflects the ethnic, religious, and socioeconomic makeup of the local population and should make a special effort to recruit a reasonable number of potentially oppressed ethnic minorities to increase their stake in fighting the insurgency."

44. *Adoo* was the common term used by SAF, BATT, and the Sultan's Firqas to refer to the enemy fighters.

45. SAF Report, "Dhofar Ops as of January 70," Thwaites Collection GB

0099, Box 1/2 LCHMA. "SAF OVERALL AIM Purely military: TO KILL THE ENEMY. No political aim aside from unconditional surrender, therefore no political or civil aids to the war. None of the established civil measures for counterinsurgency exist. a. No police or special branch; b. no resettlement of the population; c. scant food control; d. no surrender or amnesty terms; e. no psyops or propaganda; f. no hearts and minds; g. no civil govt on the Jebel; h. comparatively little intelligence."

46. Tony Jeapes, *SAS: Secret War* (Surrey: Harper Collins, 1996), 23-24.

47. Beckett, *Britain and Oman*, "The British Counter-insurgency Campaign in Dhofar," 186-187. "The field craft, ambush skills, and sniping of the insurgents … [*adoo*] … were generally excellent. They were wholly familiar with the terrain, and were highly mobile. Increasingly, too, they had become supplied with modern Soviet and Chinese weapons. … The standard of insurgent training, however, varied, and the *adoo*'s performance with mortars and recoilless rifles could be erratic … they much preferred a stand-off encounter … in daylight … [using] darkness for movement or laying mines … rarely capable of holding ground … seeking instead to dominate the jebel by their mobility."

48. McKeown, *Britain and Oman*, 44. After a failed operation to capture the caves at Shershitti, the Muscat Regiment under the command of Colonel Peter Thwaites abandoned the western area to the enemy. This left Rakhyut open to attack and overrun.

49. Sibley, *A Monk in the SAS*, 297-298.

50. McKeown, *Britain and Oman*, 44.

51. Ladwig, *Supporting Allies in COIN*, 70. "Paranoid about the prospect of another uprising in Northern Oman, he [Sultan Taimur] mandated that at least one battalion of the SAF remain in the north at all times."

52. Akehurst, *We Won a War*, 33-34. "There were four Omani infantry battalions, the Muscat Regiment …, the Northern Frontier Regiment …, the Desert Regiment …, and the Jebel Regiment … Two of these would be in Dhofar at any one time, on nine month tours, while the other two would be in their permanent bases at Bid-Bid and Nizwa in Northern Oman, recruiting and retraining for their next Dhofar tour."

53. The Sultan's enemies tried three separate attempts to shift focus and forces from Dhofar to Northern Oman by conducting or plotting to conduct attacks in the north in 1970, 1972, and 1974 (as discussed later in this chapter).

54. Sibley, *A Monk in the SAS*, 298.

55. Bryan Ray, *Dangerous Frontier:, Campaigning in Somaliland & Oman*, (South Yorkshire: Pen & Sword, 2008), 127-128.

56. Ladwig, *Supporting Allies in COIN*, 71. "Sultan Said's fears of a northern uprising proved justified. In June 1970, a group of Omani exiles calling itself the National Democratic Front for the Liberation of Oman and the Arabian Gulf attacked several northern towns. Although they were quickly defeated, the revolt made it clear how isolated and unpopular Sultan Said was."

57. Ladwig, *Supporting Allies in COIN*, 84-85. Found in endnote 59.

58. Ladwig, *Supporting Allies in COIN*, 71.

59. BL070, Retired General Officer. Interview by Mark Battjes, Ben Boardman, Robert Green, Richard Johnson, Aaron Kaufman, Dustin Mitchell, Nathan Springer, and Thomas Walton, 30 March 2011.

60. Beckett, "The British Counter-insurgency Campaign in Dhofar," 179. "Within 24 hours, Qaboos established an Interim Advisory Council, which invited Qaboos's exiled uncle, Sayyid Tariq bin Taimur, to become prime minister. Other exiled Omanis were also recalled. Restrictions on movements within the state and to selected foreign countries were lifted, political prisoners were released, and a development plan was announced."

61. Beckett, "The British Counter-insurgency Campaign in Dhofar," 179.

62. Ken Perkins, *A Fortunate Soldier*, (London: Brassey's Defence Publishers Limited, 1988), 119. "With the advent of Sultan Qaboos, civil development was begun in earnest and the oil revenues, hitherto unused, were deployed to hustle Oman into the twentieth century."

63. Ladwig, *Supporting Allies in COIN*, 71.

64. BL070, Retired General Officer.

65. Tony Jeapes, *SAS: Operation Oman.* (London: William Kimber, 1980), 31.

66. BL070, Retired General Officer.

67. Sibley, *A Monk in the SAS*, 299.

68. Jeapes, *SAS: Operation Oman*, 28.

69. Beckett, "The British Counter-insurgency Campaign in Dhofar," 182. "The shift to Marxism within PFLOAG undermined the two fundamental principles of jebeli life — Islam and tribalism. This occurred to such an extent that 24 of the most experienced former DLF insurgents, led by Salim Mubarak, surrendered to the SAF following a gun battle with hard line elements."

70. BL330, SAS Dhofar veteran. According to an SAS Dhofar veteran present at the time of Mubarak's surrender, Mubarak could not surrender to the army and therefore surrendered to a British Army Training Team with about 100 men. The difference may be that among the approximately 100 men, 24 were some of his most experienced fighters. "He couldn't surrender to Jaysh [army] so he surrendered to BATT, British Army Training Team. While arrangements were being made for his, if you like, more formal type of reception, he stayed the night with me... he surrendered with this whole firqa, a group of about a hundred, and he'd left them at memorial gardens which was about ten miles away, and walked in himself."

71. Jeapes, *SAS: Operation Oman*, 28.

72. BL070, Retired General Officer. Cites Salim Mubarak as saying, "We are going to form a firqa of all the people coming down [from the Jebel to join the Sultan] ... and then we will sweep them [*adoo*] off the Jebel!"

73. BL070, Retired General Officer.

74. Akehurst, *We Won a War*, 61. "The first Firqat to be formed was multi-

tribal and failed for this reason. The Jebali people were intensely tribal and very jealous of their own tribe's lands and customs. Subsequent Firqats were therefore always tribal."

75. Sibley, *A Monk in the SAS*, 299.

76. Irregular Forces – SAF View, Annex A to Section 10 of unknown report, Middle East Centre, St. Anthony's College, Oxford, UK, p. 2.

77. Akehurst, *We Won a War*, 42. "Finally, in the Dhofar Brigade, there were the Firqats. In mid-1974 there were about 1,000 of them, and more joined every week. Mostly they were surrendered enemy who after interrogation (a relaxed and friendly process in the company of former colleagues) were given a cooling-off period of perhaps a month and then, if they wished, allowed to join their tribal Firqat."

78. BL050, Dhofar Veterans Panel. Interview by Mark Battjes, Ben Boardman, Robert Green, Richard Johnson, Aaron Kaufman, Dustin Mitchell, Nathan Springer, and Thomas Walton, 38 March 2011.

79. BL070, Retired General Officer.

80. Gardiner, *In the Service of the Sultan*, 156.

81. Beckett, "The British Counter-insurgency Campaign in Dhofar," 185. "A key ingredient to this expansion was the recruitment of seconded and contracted British military officers with the correct background and mindset."

82. Beckett, "The British Counter-insurgency Campaign in Dhofar," 185.

83. Akehurst, *We Won a War*, 32.

84. Gardiner, *In the Service of the Sultan*, 159

85. Akehurst, *We Won a War*, 43.

86. BL330, SAS Dhofar veteran. "The next year was about, if you like, establishing the firqas, and then in '71 was Operation JAGUAR which was the first operation for two years for the jaysh to re-establish a presence on the Jebel. That was led by two squadrons of SAS and certainly the three original firqas ... with B Squadron coming in with FKW from the north, and G Squadron coming up from Marbat ... That was achieved basically, and a foot hold was established on the Jebel. We then split into two groups, one to the west and one to the east of Wadi Darbat. The jaysh came in and consolidated the positions, and then we just sat there for the next few months while the *adoo* came and threw everything they could at us to try and dislodge us. Every night there were pitched battles and contacts which really made a lot of noise but achieved very little as far as the *adoo* were concerned. I think we took a few casualties but nothing major. And then of course we used to patrol out during the day with the firqa, and the jaysh used to hold the ground. That was the pattern if you like for the next year. So, I can't remember exactly when it was in '71, but Operation JAGUAR was the big operation to re-establish a presence, a government presence, right on the Jebel, and that was successful. And the next seven years we spent moving slowly westwards."

87. Another significant event in 1971 was the arrival of the first element of Iranian forces fighting in support of the Sultan. The Iranian forces would

play a key role in the campaign. Not only did their presence signal international support for the Sultan of Oman, they also assumed static defensive positions in the Western Area of Dhofar which allowed SAF to concentrate in the Eastern and Central Areas. Iranian forces would re-open the Midway Road and recapture the coastal town of Rakhyut. Part of their defensive efforts included constructing the Damavand Line which ran north from the coastal town of Rakhyut.

88. Akehurst, *We Won a War*, 61. "The Firqats at that time were about 1,400 strong and were the key to the centre and east. Considerable strength would be needed to take on the enemy in the west and it could only be amassed at the expense of the centre and east. Either the enemy must be cleaned out altogether, an impossible task in the short term, or the securing must be taken over by the Firqats. If roads could be built to those places now supplied by air, especially helicopters, more resources still would be made available for the west."

89. Irregular Forces – SAF View, Annex A to Section 10 General Graham Papers, Middle East Centre, St. Anthony's College, Oxford, UK, p. 4. "In the early days when a small highly selective force was envisaged it was agreed to pay Firqats SAF pay plus ten Riyals per month."

90. Irregular Forces – SAF View, 1.

91. Irregular Forces – SAF View, 1.

92. Akehurst, *We Won a War*, 81. "It was felt to be a wiser policy to keep the Firqats in the smaller tribal groups responsible for the security of their own homes and tribal areas but without integral heavy weapons or support weapons. Although this would mean up to 3,000 of them being paid for not much work, and in some cases no work at all, it represented good security at reasonable cost, besides being a very satisfactory means of distributing some of the national wealth among the jebel tribes — an interesting form of social security."

93. BATT Notes on Raising and Training of Irregular Forces in Dhofar, Annex B to Section 10 of unknown report, Middle East Centre, St. Anthony's College, Oxford, UK, p. 1.

94. BATT Notes, 1.

95. Beckett, "The British Counter-insurgency Campaign in Dhofar," 187.

96. British Army Tactical Doctrine Retrieval Cell, Notes from a group of presentations on Dhofar, (Alanbrooke Hall, Staff College, UK: 30 June 1982), 2.

97. Beckett, "The British Counter-insurgency Campaign in Dhofar," 188.

98. Sibley, *A Monk in the SAS*, 301.

99. BL070, Retired General Officer.

100. Sibley, *A Monk in the SAS*, 301.

101. Sibley, *A Monk in the SAS*, 301.

102. Price, *Oman: Insurgency and Development*, 4. "From 1965 to 1967 the DLF's main objective was to consolidate and establish its presence in Dhofar. Dividing the province into three sections — eastern, western, and central — it recruited volunteers on an individual basis."

103. Ray, *Dangerous Frontiers*, 128-129.

104. Sibley, *A Monk in the SAS*, 301.

105. British Army Tactical Doctrine Retrieval Cell, Notes from a group of presentations on Dhofar, (Alanbrooke Hall, Staff College, UK: 30 June 1982), 3.

106. British Army Tactical Doctrine Retrieval Cell, Notes from a group of presentations on Dhofar, (Alanbrooke Hall, Staff College, UK: 30 June 1982), 4.

107. British Army Tactical Doctrine Retrieval Cell, Notes from a group of presentations on Dhofar, (Alanbrooke Hall, Staff College, UK: 30 June 1982), 6-7.

108. British Army Tactical Doctrine Retrieval Cell, Notes from a group of presentations on Dhofar, (Alanbrooke Hall, Staff College, UK: 30 June 1982), 7.

109. Beckett, "The British Counter-insurgency Campaign in Dhofar," 188.

110. O'Neill, "Revolutionary War in Oman," 225.

111. Beckett, "The British Counter-insurgency Campaign in Dhofar," 188.

112. Beckett, "The British Counter-insurgency Campaign in Dhofar," 188.

113. Akehurst, *We Won a War*, 36.

114. Akehurst, *We Won a War*, 33.

115. Akehurst, *We Won a War*, 35-36.

116. Akehurst, *We Won a War*, 42.

117. Akehurst, *We Won a War*, 61.

118. Akehurst, *We Won a War*, 61-62.

119. Akehurst, *We Won a War*, 63-64. The full pattern devised by Brigadier Akehurst was, "1. A SAF operation in strength supported by a Firqat secures a position of the Firqat's choice which dominated its tribal area. 2. Military engineers build a track to the position giving road access, followed by an airstrip if possible. 3. A drill is brought down the track followed by a Civil Action Team with shop, school, clinic, and mosque. 4. SAF thins out to the minimum needed to provide security. 5. Water is pumped to the surface and into the distribution system prepared by military engineers to offer storage points for humans, and troughs for animals. 6. Civilians come in from miles around and talk to Firqat, SAF and Government representatives. They are told that enemy activity in the area will result in the water being cut off. 7. Civilians move out in surrounding area and tell the enemy not to interfere with what is obviously 'a good thing.' 8. Enemy, very dependent on civilians, stop all aggressive action and either go elsewhere or hide. 9. Tribal area is secure. 10. All SAF withdrawn."

120. Akehurst, *We Won a War*, 75. "During October [1974] the policy of installing Firqats in their tribal areas really got under way. One of the first, and most difficult, was at Hagleet, near Ayun, just north of the monsoon-affected jebel. This had been a beleaguered defensive position in the early days of the war from which SAF had eventually withdrawn. As always happened, the enemy laid antipersonnel mines in and around the sangars but here they were more prolific and better hidden than usual. In the first two days three Jebel Regiment soldiers were badly wounded and one slightly. It was decided to move to virgin ground two miles away. The other moves went without a hitch and both Firqats

and civilians were delighted. New positions were established at Zeak, Ashinhaib, Ayun, Burg Haluf, and Jebel Khaftawt, where a five-kilometre line to interrupt enemy movement was constructed by the Jebel Regiment and called 'Hammer'. It was almost due north of Raysut and a major blow to the enemy who had been using the area for years as a sort of holiday camp for rest and recuperation."

121. Sibley, *A Monk in the SAS*, 304.

122. Akehurst, *We Won a War*, 75. "New positions were established at Zeak, Ashinhaib, Ayun, Burg Haluf, and Jebel Khaftawt, where a five-kilometre line to interrupt enemy movement was constructed by the Jebel Regiment and called 'Hammer.' It was almost due north of Raysut and a major blow to the enemy who had been using the area for years as a sort of holiday camp for rest and recuperation."

123. Akehurst, *We Won a War*, 77. "The Frontier Force mounted a major operation at the end of October [1974] to tackle the enemy south and east of Tawi Atair, with the bonus of opening the road from Taqa to Marbat which had been closed for so long. ... The installation of the Firqats in their tribal areas was beginning to pay off already, with the number of surrenders increasing dramatically and the flow of information from both Firqats and civilians providing invaluable intelligence. This confirmed that lack of supplies was causing severe morale problems among the enemy in the centre. The new positions also made valuable patrol bases deep in what had been enemy-held areas. These successes led to more ambitious plans to expand the track network on the jebel."

124. Akehurst, *We Won a War*, 80. "In November, at the Sultan's invitation, Sir Gawain Bell and Mr. Tony Ashworth, a British Government official, came to Dhofar to study the long-term needs of the province." Part of their report included recommendations on what to do with the *firqa*.

125. Akehurst, *We Won a War*, 81. "The report suggested that Firqats should be formed into a National Guard which would be multi-tribal and firmly under discipline. This plan was examined in great detail during the following months, and retained its adherents, but was shelved for the time being because of the practical difficulties of selling it to the Firqats and of arranging the expensive and intensive training for such a force. The Jebali is not easily dragooned into anything and would not take kindly to being taken far from home for disciplined military training. But far from home it would have to be or the disruption and absenteeism would be intolerable. There might also be a potential security risk in creating a force of this kind with modern training and weapons when in the previous year or two many of the tribesmen involved had been fighting against the Government and had been subject to Communist indoctrination."

126. Akehurst, *We Won a War*, 81. "It was felt to be a wiser policy to keep the Firqats in the smaller tribal groups responsible for the security of their own homes and tribal areas but without integral heavy weapons or support weapons. Although this would mean up to 3,000 of them being paid for not much work, and in some cases no work at all, it represented good security at reasonable cost, besides being a very satisfactory means of distributing some of the national wealth among the jebel tribes - an interesting form of social security." p. 81

127. British Army Tactical Doctrine Retrieval Cell, Notes from a group of

presentations on Dhofar, (Alanbrooke Hall, Staff College, UK: 30 June 1982), 4.

128. Akehurst, *We Won a War*, 88. General Creasy, CSAF, visited the Dhofar Brigade on his way to meet with the Iranians, and to discuss options for how the Dhofar Brigade could take on the mission at Sherishitti. CSAF believed the Iranians would succeed in their ongoing operation to capture the town of Rakhyut, but still had a great deal of work to do. After two hours of planning, Akehurst and his staff determined that the task would have to fall on the Jebel Regiment of the Dhofar Brigade.

129. Jeapes, *SAS: Secret War*, 200.

130. BL070, Retired General Officer. The original intent behind raising *firqas* was to create multi-tribal units in order to create a balance of power and avoid tribal based units. Although the *firqa* Saladdin was multi-tribal, they were held together by their leader Salim Mubarak. Upon his death, a BATT officer appointed Mubarak's second in command to lead the *firqa*. This person was rejected by the *firqa*, which lead to its disintegration.

131. Akehurst, *We Won a War*, 91. "Now began an appalling and frustrating delay from which we learned a valuable lesson for the rest of the campaign. Quite wrongly as it turned out, but for what seemed sensible reasons at the time, it had been decided to lead the advance with a mixed group of Firqats. ... They had been assembled hurriedly from different Firqats which made for a lack of cohesion and they now applied deliberate delaying tactics."

132. Ray, *Dangerous Frontiers*, 190.

133. British Army Tactical Retrieval Cell, Notes from a group of presentations on Dhofar, Alanbrooke Hall, Staff College, UK (30 June 1982), 5.

134. Akehurst, *We Won a War*, 139.

135. Akehurst, *We Won a War*, 69. Probably the South Mahra Firqa. "An important early move was to install thirty men of the South Mahra Firqat at Sarfait. This was their tribal area and they made a significant contribution to the pioneering of routes off the position, which was required of the battalion by my first operational order. They knew them intimately and behaved with commendable courage and aggression as they picked their way through the minefields."

136. Akehurst, *We Won a War*, 157-158. "The prize was great. If we moved down to the bottom and held on we could stop all enemy supplies and movement of men and material, which would quickly end the war. ... As we talked about these things and were approaching a decision there was a call from Ian on the National radio from down below: 'I've just told the Firqats that we are only staying for two or three days and they are very *mush mabsoot* [unhappy]. They say we must stay and we can make it very difficult for the enemy. If we try to withdraw I think there may be a rebellion.' If the scales needed tipping this tipped them. If the Firqats wanted to stay it was likely to be all right."

137. Ken Perkins, *A Fortunate Soldier* (London: Brassey's Defence Publishers Limited, 1988), 147. "On the morning of the 16th, still with five days to go to the main operation, I arrived at Salalah en route to visit Ian's company, anticipating that I might have to fly in between shot and shell. I was met by John Akehurst who reported that while the enemy were still making life hazardous on

Sarfait, they had so far ignored our diversion. He thought we should reinforce success and, in anticipation of my approval, had scratched together an ad hoc force as there would not be time to assemble the intended D-Day battalions which were still deployed in the Salalah area. As we drove the few hundred yards to John Akehurst's headquarters I made the decision to switch the main operation to Sarfait that night and out of the window went months of planning . . ."

138. Sibley, *A Monk in the SAS*, 306.

139. Akehurst, *We Won a War*, 173.

140. Jeapes, *SAS: Secret War*, 230.

141. Jeapes, *SAS: Secret War*, 237.

142. Jeapes, *SAS: Operation Oman*, 31.

143. De La Billiere, *Looking for Trouble*, 266-267.

144. Ladwig, *Supporting Allies in COIN*, 80. "In a counterinsurgency, the armed forces of the host nation should bear the brunt of the fighting. In providing personnel, the British kept that point in mind as they focused on supplying capabilities and expertise lacked by the Omanis. Despite the need for large numbers of combat troops, the British declined to provide regular soldiers for combat operations in Oman. This had two effects. First, it required Oman to provide its own soldiery, which it did by tripling the size of the SAF between 1970 and 1972. Second, when this proved insufficient, Oman reached out to regional allies. The deployment of combat troops from a Muslim country like Iran was far more politically acceptable than British troops would have been. Tangible support from Jordan and Iran also helped deflect criticism, particularly from the Soviets and the political left in Britain, that the British were engaged in a neo-colonial enterprise or that Oman was simply a puppet state."

145. Jeapes, *SAS: Secret War*, 14.

146. Jeapes, *SAS: Secret War*, 239-240. "Before becoming commissar of this unit, he had taught political affairs at the Lenin School at Al Ghayda and before that he had been in charge of political broadcasting on Radio Aden."

147. Akehurst, *We Won a War*, 61. "The Firqats at that time were about 1,400 strong and were the key to the centre and east. Considerable strength would be needed to take on the enemy in the west and it could only be amassed at the expense of the centre and east. Either the enemy must be cleaned out altogether, an impossible task in the short term, or the securing must be taken over by the Firqats. If roads could be built to those places now supplied by air, especially helicopters, more resources still would be made available for the west."

148. Akehurst, *We Won a War*, 43. "I have described the Jebali as fierce, independent and unruly and these qualities were much in evidence in the Firqats, who were very difficult indeed to control. . . . Properly motivated, and with the prospect of financial or other gain, they could be splendid fighters, as good for us as they had been against us; but equally they could, if the mood took them, be intransigent and uncooperative, sometimes aggressively so. . . . Again, however, I must reiterate how vitally important the Firqats were in the struggle. Their knowledge of the ground and their influence with the civilians were indispensible,

and worth all the time, trouble and money spent to secure and retain their goodwill and allegiance."

149. BL330, Interview with SAS Dhofar veteran. "The firqa leaders used to come into the BATT conference. We used to run a firqa leader conference. The CO from Hereford used to come out and we would have a conference with the firqa leaders. … It was a regular thing. Probably towards the end of each four month tour I suspect. [Did those influence operations in any way?] Oh I think so, yes. It was a one-to-one with the CO of the Regiment, I don't think any jaysh were present, but it was a one to one thing with the firqa and the BATT. We would say what we wanted and they would say what they wanted."

150. Akehurst, *We Won a War*, 61-62. "The first Firqat to be formed was multi-tribal and failed for this reason. The Jebali people were intensely tribal and very jealous of their own tribe's lands and customs. Subsequent Firquats were therefore always tribal. Several Firqats were formed from surrendered enemy but had to live on the Salalah Plain or in other secure areas not their own because the enemy prevented occupation of their tribal areas. From conversations with their leaders and their SAS advisers I learned of their intense desire to reoccupy their own land. All of them promised instant security if they could be established in positions of their own choosing."

151. While the Watt's plan called for raising indigenous forces to fight for the Sultan, there was no clear plan of how to do this or what the indigenous force would look like. The surrender of Salim Mubarak and his firqa came as a surprise to all. As mentioned earlier, the formation of firqa to fight for the Sultan was Mubarak's idea.

152. Gardiner, *In the Service of the Sultan*, 159. "… the concept of recruiting the Firqat and keeping them alongside was a courageous masterstroke, generally attributed to John Watts in 1970 when he was the Commanding Officer of the SAS."

153. There was at the time a psychological operations campaign which emphasized the Sultan's offer of amnesty.

154. BL330, SAS Dhofar veteran.

155. BL330, SAS Dhofar veteran. "On an operation, branching out from our main base to see first of all what the lay of the land was, and what we could establish, and again whether we could get SEPs in. They came in in a steady trickle."

156. Akehurst, *We Won a War*, 61-62.

157. Gardiner, *In the Service of the Sultan*, 159. "They were, therefore, extremely useful in retaining the peace in an area which had been cleared of *adoo*, thereby leaving conventional forces to get on with prosecuting the war elsewhere. For all their limitations, I do not believe we could have won the war without the Firqat."

158. Gardiner, *In the Service of the Sultan*, 159. "As our former enemies they knew the ground and the tactics of their former friends intimately, and they were good at things that we were poor at, namely reconnaissance, gathering intelligence and communicating with the nomadic population. They were of that population after all."

159. McKeown, *Britain and Oman*, 45.

160. Sibley, *A Monk in the SAS*, 299.

161. BI050, Dhofar Veterans Panel.

162. Jeapes, *SAS: Secret War*, 14.

163. Irregular Forces – SAF View, 2.

164. Irregular Forces – SAF View, 3. "Firqats have weapons similar to SAF rifle platoons. They are not armed with GPMGs or 81mm mortars as a matter of principle." The firqa relied on BATT for these types of supporting weapons.

165. Irregular Forces – SAF View, 3.

166. Gardiner, *In the Service of the Sultan*, 156.

167. Akehurst, *We Won a War*, 177.

168. Irregular Forces – SAF View, Annex A to Section 10 General Graham Papers, Middle East Centre, St. Anthony's College, Oxford, UK, p. 3. "Each Firqat usually elects two leaders: a military leader to lead them in the field, and a tribal political leader who is the more powerful to decide all major matters."

169. BL330, SAS Dhofar veteran. "Basically because, I didn't make this point earlier but, you had a firqa leader, an Arab firqa leader who was from the tribe but when BATT was with the firqa it was the BATT commander who was the firqa leader. So when I was with the firqa I was the firqa leader, and that was true of all the BATT/firqa relationships. So you were actually in command, and what you said was an order even though perhaps there was some negotiation before you would go firm on that."

170. Jeapes, *SAS: Secret War*, 41. Jeapes referring to Salim Mubarak: "I was naively surprised and impressed by the speed with which he understood the reasoning behind information services, not yet knowing that in the coming months I was to learn more from him that I could teach."

171. McKeown, *Britain and Oman*, 97-99. "The first, and fundamental, factor in winning the Dhofar War was the change of Sultan in 1970." "The policy of welcoming back former enemy without fear of punishment was very important in giving members of the PLA a way out. ... This led to a constant drain of defectors from the Front which increased where government military pressure reduced their morale."

172. BL330, SAS Dhofar veteran.

173. Akehurst, *We Won a War*, 29. "Until 1972 China had provided a good deal of support, but was then persuaded by the Shah to desist, agreeing because of its economic and cultural interests in Iran. Russia then became the dominant supporter, although Libya and Cuba also sent money, supplies and training staff."

174. Jeapes, *SAS: Secret War*, 24. "Whereas SAF, too, were still largely armed with the old .303 bolt-action British Enfield rifle and only just beginning to re-equip with automatic FNs, the hard-core *adoo* all had modern, fully automatic Soviet Kalashnikov assault rifles and machine guns, and even the soft-core had Simonov semi-automatic. Nor did their weapons stop at small arms. The Chinese 82mm mortar, for instance, is not only very effective, but cleverly designed

too. It will fire the bombs of the British 81mm mortar besides its own, whereas Chinese bombs will not fit into the British barrel. The 60mm mortar is smaller, but outranges by far its British equivalent."

175. BL330, SAS Dhofar veteran. "FTZ were in the west without BATT and they asked for BATT, which I translated at the time. We were extended two weeks in our tour in order to go down to the west to conduct an operation with the firqa, FTZ, Tariq bin Zaid, which then led on to the disastrous operation in the Shershitti area. They had operated without BATT for some time, and they particularly wanted BATT."

176. Akehurst, *We Won a War*, 36. "Fire response was always quick and accurate, and often very close indeed; it gave SAF an important advantage."

177. Ladwig, *Supporting Allies in COIN*, 67. "The best among them [PFLOAG members] were sent to China for specialized military training at the Anti-Imperialist School in Beijing …"

178. British Army Tactical Doctrine Retrieval Cell, Anti-Guerrilla Operations in Dhofar Lessons Learned, 23-24. This document describes the PFLOAG course of instruction at the Anti-Imperialist School in Peking, China. "The course is of 6 months duration. It alternates between one month's Political Instruction, the next Military Instruction." The document includes the titles of the courses for both political and military instruction as well as a daily routine for students.

179. Jeapes, *SAS: Secret War*, 71-76.

180. Jeapes, *SAS: Secret War*, 76.

181. BL330, SAS Dhofar veteran. "There was a clash between communism and Islam. And also, as I said earlier, the communists overplayed their hand. They thought they had control, and they did. They had about a 90-plus percent control over the people on the Jebel. But they'd just overplayed that extra 5 percent perhaps, and started intimidating and bullying, and I think they tried to remove the tribal structure, and they put in place a typically Russian-type political hierarchy which is unacceptable to the Dhofaris."

Chapter 4
Operation IRAQI FREEDOM Case Study

During Operation IRAQI FREEDOM, the US military and coaltion partners raised several types of security forces to include army, police, national guard, and irregular security forces. The manner in which the US-led coalition raised these security forces was as haphazard as its overall strategy, and indicated poor planning and preparation for post-combat operations. This chapter will discuss the pre-invasion planning, key strategy shifts, and the irregular security forces of the Anbar Awakening and the Sons of Iraq program.[1]

Plans and Strategy

Since the defeat of Saddam Hussein's forces in the 1991 Persian Gulf War, United Nations members had maintained no-fly zones in the northern and southern portions of Iraq to limit Saddam's brutality against minority groups within the country.[2] No-fly zones supported the US strategy to contain Saddam's regime versus toppling it, which would possibly draw the US into a lengthy internal struggle.[3] The Clinton administration continued the Bush policy of containing Saddam, and ordered a massive airstrike against suspected weapons storage locations after tension over Saddam's lack of compliance with United Nations' weapons inspectors grew beyond an acceptable level.[4]

With a defiant Saddam Hussein still in power, the US military developed contingency plans as a preparation for possible future hostile action by Iraqi forces. General Binford Peay, Commander of US Central Command (CENTCOM), developed an operations plan (OPLAN) to counter what he termed a "Basra breakout" in which Saddam would mass five divisions in southern Iraq and overwhelm the forces defending Kuwait, requiring basically a replay of the 1991 campaign to oust Iraqi forces from Kuwait.[5]

Known as CENTCOM OPLAN 1003-98, successive CENTCOM Commanders, including US Marine Corps General Anthony Zinni and U.S. Army General Tommy Franks, updated the plan for war with Iraq. Citing an interview with Zinni, Gordon and Trainor offer the following insight regarding refinement of OPLAN 1003-98:

> "If I had to point to one person who was deeply involved in 1003-98 it was Tommy Franks," Zinni recalled. "He was the major contributor to the force levels and the planning and everything else. He was more involved in it than just about anybody else. That was his life. He and his planning staff seemed to be committed to the plan."[6]

OPLAN 1003-98, updated by Franks as the commander of Third Army (the Army portion of CENTCOM),[7] and endorsed by Zinni, focused more on the aftermath of the collapse of Saddam's regime than on the conventional fight required to defeat Saddam's forces.[8] With the security, stability, and reconstruction seen as the more difficult part of the problem, OPLAN 1003-98 called for more than 400,000 troops. Although Franks moved from command of Third Army to command of CENTCOM,[9] he later found his own plan inadequate when briefing the Secretary of Defense, Donald Rumsfeld.[10] At some point it appeared that Franks' focus shifted from the requirements for post-regime collapse to the requirements to cause the regime to collapse.

As planning and preparations progressed to support a possible conflict with Iraq, OPLAN 1003-98 became OPLAN 1003V, no longer a conceptual plan but an active one.[11] Although the interaction between Secretary Rumsfeld and General Franks was described as "constant negotiation,"[12] Rumsfeld got what he wanted in the way of decreased troop commitments (he wanted a plan for 125,000 troops) for operations in Iraq.[13] A coalition led and predominately composed of US forces invaded Iraq in 2003 to enforce United Nations Security Council Resolutions[14] which required Iraq to provide full disclosure of its weapons of mass destruction program.[15] The aim of the operation was to topple the regime of Saddam Hussein, hopefully engendering a popular uprising which would take control from the Baath Party and pursue a democratic form of government.[16]

The war began on 19 March 2003 with an air campaign two days after President Bush issued an ultimatum for Saddam and his sons to leave Iraq or face military action.[17] In the end, counting Gulf State Coalition allied contributions, the coalition invaded Iraq with 292,000 troops, 170,000 of which were ground troops.[18] As a former battalion commander in Iraq commented, the US-led coalition lost control because efficiency trumped effectiveness: "We would have saved ourselves a number of years and lives if we had committed the large force early vice doing it on the cheap."[19]

Many have criticized the invasion of Iraq as having neglected planning and preparation for post-regime collapse. Although Franks' self-proclaimed grand strategy based on "lines" of operation and "slices" or elements of Saddam's power and control included nonkinetic considerations such as infrastructure, civilian population, political-military, and civil-military lines and slices, it amounted to little in the way of actual preparation for the post-combat phase.[20] Ultimately the job of planning for post-combat phase operations fell to retired Army Lieutenant General Jay Garner, whom Rumsfeld appointed as "… our senior man in charge of Iraqi occupation and reconstruction …"[21]

Franks acknowledges that appointing Garner to lead the post-combat phase was important, but not enough. In order to succeed in his mission, Garner would require a secure environment in order to conduct civil action. Additionally Franks noted, "Washington would be responsible for providing the policy – and, I hoped, sufficient resources – to win the hearts and minds of the Iraqi people …"[22] In the end, possibly the greatest challenge Garner faced was unity of command. As Bing West noted in his book *The Strongest Tribe,*

> Once the war was over, he [Franks] and Secretary of Defense Rumsfeld had agreed that retired Army Lt. Gen. Jay Garner would serve as the Central Command deputy for Phase IV – the occupation of Iraq. Yet when fighting petered out in late April, the Phase III commander for combat operations, Lt. Gen. David McKiernan, kept control over all units. Central Command never passed control from Phase III to Phase IV. Garner was supposedly in charge, but the 173,000 soldiers in the invincible coalition did not work for him. He was stranded in Baghdad, his tiny staff out of touch and having to hitch rides to meetings. Garner was a deputy commander with no one to command.[23]

Although it had been the stated policy of the US to "seek to remove the Saddam Hussein regime from power in Iraq and to replace it with a democratic government" since 1998, the focus of planning and preparation for OPLAN 1003V seemed to emphasize the removal of Saddam and neglect the formation of a democratic government part of the policy.[24]

Perhaps part of the problem US planners had in preparing for post-combat or Phase IV operations was the prevailing sentiment that the associated tasks were *postwar* issues. As Nadia Schadlow argued in "War and the Art of Governance,"

> The root of Washington's failure to anticipate the political disorder in Iraq rests precisely in the characterization of these challenges as "postwar" problems, a characterization used by virtually all analysts inside and outside of government. The Iraq situation is only the most recent example of the reluctance of civilian and military leaders, as well as most outside experts, to consider the establishment of political and economic order as *a part of war itself.*[25]

Franks wrote, "Throughout our planning of 1003V, we discussed Phase IV – 'the Day After.' A postwar Iraq might be modeled on post-World War II Japan or Germany."[26] Franks plan for Phase IV was called Eclipse II after the postwar Eclipse plan for Germany.[27] In postwar Japan and Germany, the economic and political recovery tasks fell to the Army as it was the only entity with the capacity to accomplish them.[28] If postwar occupation of Japan and Germany were the models Franks used for his Phase IV plan, it seems odd that he accepted a force cap so far below his own estimates of the number required to secure a post-Saddam Iraq.

Another potential cause for the lack of planning and preparation for Phase IV was an institutional bias toward fighting at the expense of post-combat operations. As Bing West described it, "For decades, the military had designed force-planning guidance that emphasized fighting and swiftly winning a major war, then withdrawing quickly to ready to fight somewhere else. This planning method ensured that the budget went to the fighting forces, while ignoring the forces needed for an occupation."[29]

Regardless of the causes of the lack of planning and preparation for Phase IV, the results were chaos, inaction, and confusion.[30] As noted in *Cobra II*, "There was a vicious circularity to the military and civilian planning. CENTCOM was hoping that the success of Garner's team would speed the withdrawal of U.S. troops; Garner was hoping that CENTCOM would provide the security he needed ..."[31] To make matters worse, Garner, who had developed a plan for Phase IV operations but was not supported in his efforts, was replaced by L. Paul Bremer III only three weeks after arriving in Iraq.[32] Bremer made two key decisions shortly thereafter. The first decision was to remove all senior government officials with ties to the Baath party. The second decision was to disband all security forces.[33] As noted in *On Point II*,

> These orders, designed to signal the end of Saddam's tyranny and the beginning of a new era, removed thousands of Sunni Arab Iraqis from political power, creating the perception that Sunni Arabs would have limited power in a new Iraq, fostering a huge unemployment problem, and leaving Iraqi institutions without bureaucratic or technical leadership.[34]

Bremer's vision for the future of Iraq seemed disconnected from the CENTCOM Commander's vision for turning over control to the Iraqis. Franks recalled, "At some point I said, we can begin drawing down our force . . . our troop reductions should parallel deployment of representative, professional Iraqi security forces. Our exit strategy will be tied to effective governance by Iraqis, not to a timeline."[35] Neither of Bremer's orders contributed to the establishment of effective governance or professional Iraqi security forces. Indeed, many believed that these decisions help fan the flames of insurgency.[36] Najim al Jabouri, the former mayor of Tal Afar, offered his understanding of the impact of Bremer's orders:

> When Paul Bremer replaced Jay Garner, the Coalition Provisional Authority's first two orders were the de-Ba'athification laws and disbanding the Iraqi security services. While many in the security services were not working after the invasion, these surprising mandates agitated the Sunni community and increased the momentum to organized insurgency.[37]

Secretary Rumsfeld did not see an insurgency growing in Iraq and explained away the growing violence as the work of "dead-enders."[38] Not until July did the new CENTCOM Commander, General John Abizaid, identify the resistance as "a classical guerrilla-type campaign."[39] The military commander in Iraq, Lieutenant General Ricardo Sanchez, presided over a broad array of approaches to the problems in Iraq. These approaches included the 3d Infantry Division's firm but even approach in Al Anbar, the 4th Infantry Division's targeting and raiding approach to eliminate insurgents, the 101st Air Assault Division's focus on restoring normalcy in Mosul through projects and engagement with local leaders and former military officers,[40] and a more traditional tactical counterinsurgency approach in southern Iraq by the British.[41] From the tactical (division) level to the strategic (Secretary of Defense) level there was no coherent plan or strategy to guide the efforts of the coalition forces.

David Galula described this kind of circumstance as an "*accidental mosaic*"[42] brought about by an absence of control over the campaign. Galula argued that control and progress go hand in hand in counterinsurgency operations using a planned execution of logical steps to guide the actions at tactical level to achieve intermediate objectives.[43] Galula emphasized the role of commanders in assessing the situation and making adjustments to adapt:

> With the step-by-step approach, the counterinsurgent provides himself with a way of assessing at any time the situation and the progress made. He can thus exert his control and conduct the war by switching means from an advanced area to a retarded one, by giving larger responsibilities to the subordinate leaders who have proved successful, and by removing those who have failed. In other words, he can command because he can verify.[44]

Without a coherent plan to apply and adapt, Sanchez was unable to grasp the situation or devise a strategy to deal with the growing violence and unrest and to guide and unify the actions of his subordinate commanders.

As violence increased across most of Iraq, the majority of coalition forces responded with blunt force,[45] perhaps in the belief that if they could crush the insurgents just a little more they would cease to be a threat. In the absence of a coherent strategy, the coalition was vulnerable to overreaction and excessive use of force which was the most readily available tool (if not the only one). For example, after the killing and mutilation of four American contractors in Fallujah, the Bush administration ordered an assault on the city against the recommendations of the CENTCOM Commander.[46] Lieutenant General James Conway, the commander of the Marine Expeditionary Force in Iraq commented, "By attacking frontally, we unified the city against us."[47] In fact, the attack on Fallujah united the greater Sunni population against the coalition forces as they saw the offensive not as an effort to bring the perpetrators of the attack on the contractors to justice but as an assault on Sunni society.[48]

The offensive, begun on 4 April 2004, ended on 9 April after two members of the Iraqi Governing Council resigned in protest of the attack.[49] Coinciding with the offensive in Fallujah was an uprising of disaffected Shia, predominately poor males, led by Muqtada al Sadr who fanned the flames against the presense of US forces in Iraq.[50] In light of the growing unrest and violence, the need for a new strategy became increasingly clear.[51]

Shifting Strategy

As Secretary of State Condoleezza Rice testified to Congress in October 2005, the US strategy in 2003 was to enforce the United Nations' resolutions against Iraq and overthrow Saddam Hussein. In 2004 the strategy shifted to executing a plan to end the occupation and establish Iraqi sovereignty. In 2005 the strategy shifted to emphasize transition, both military and political, to an Iraqi-led campaign. In 2006 US strategy would shift to clear, hold, build to create lasting stability in Iraq.[52] As Galula pointed out, "All wars are theoretically fought for a political purpose, although in some cases the final political outcome differs greatly from the one intended initially."[53] These shifts in strategy could be indicative of the administration's reaction to changing circumstances on the ground. Based on the lack of post-conflict planning it is difficult to give the administration credit for adapting the strategy based on an evolving situation. More likely it was a result of short-sighted efforts to plan the way ahead.

As discussed earlier, Franks saw the development of Iraqi security forces as the path to success in Iraq. Although Franks did not include countering an insurgency in his post-combat planning, all of the counterinsurgency theorists and authors discussed to this point also identified indigenous security forces as a key component of a sound counterinsurgency strategy.[54] Bremer's CPA Orders No.1 and No. 2 made this path more difficult as they eliminated a huge portion of the Iraqi population that was fit for military service, and the majority of the population with military experience (the size of the Iraqi Army which Bremer officially dissolved was estimated to have been as many as 400,000).[55] Additionally, as it became clear that the campaign in Iraq would take longer than one year, requiring a rotation of troops to replace those already in country, huge gaps in the US military force structure emerged.[56]

Even if the US could replace one-for-one the forces deployed in the invasion to continue operations through the subsequent year, the coalition force structure would have been inadequate. Carter Malkasian said of the situation, "The breadth of violence made it abundantly clear that the coalition could not secure Iraq without more numbers."[57] Indeed, Lieutenant General Sanchez determined additional forces were required to cope with the security situation in Iraq, "but at all levels of command it was acknowledged that there were no additional forces available."[58]

The only viable option to increase the size of the force in Iraq to stem the tide of the growing unrest and violence was Iraqi security forces. According to Malkasian,

> Abizaid and the American commanders had been looking

to the Iraqis to supply those numbers, rather than request US reinforcements, which was not considered politically feasible and might deepen the perception of occupation among the Iraqi population. Since the dissolution of the old Iraqi Army, the coalition had focused on creating locally based forces, known as the Iraqi Civil Defense Corps (renamed the Iraqi National Guard after June 2004), to help provide security within Iraq while a new Iraqi Army was built.[59]

Unfortunately, the Iraqi Civil Defense Corps/Iraqi National Guard produced mixed results, largely dependent on the population from which they were drawn.[60] In addition to the social pressures and perceptions, the lack of effective training and advisers contributed to the collapse of the majority of these units in the Sunni dominated areas.[61]

The stopgap measure of locally raised security forces had failed, at least in the Sunni dominated areas. Franks had predicted that the success of the campaign required professional Iraqi Army forces.[62] As Lieutenant General Conway remarked in late 2004, "The situation will change when Iraqi Army divisions arrive. They will engender people with a sense of nationalism. Together with an elected government, they will create Stability."[63] These predictions of success based on the arrival of professional Iraqi Army divisions would prove to be false as the Sunnis refused to cooperate[64] (especially against fellow Sunnis in the insurgency),[65] and Iraqi Army units of predominately Shia ethnicity were unwelcome, ineffective, and hesitant to operate in Sunni dominated areas.[66]

Perhaps the first adjustment to the strategy in Iraq could be described as accelerated democracy. As Bing West noted referring to President Bush, "Addressing the Army War College in May of 2004, he shifted the rationale for the war from removing the Saddam regime to bringing democracy to the Middle East . . . He clung to the belief that an election and an Iraqi government would reduce the insurgency and improve security by unifying the country."[67] As President Bush described it,

> Our agenda, in contrast, is freedom and independence, security and prosperity for the Iraqi people. And by removing a source of terrorist violence and instability in the Middle East, we also make our own country more secure. Our coalition has a clear goal, understood by all -- to see the Iraqi people in charge of Iraq for the first time in generations. America's task in Iraq is not only to defeat an enemy, it is to give strength to a friend - a free, representative government that serves its people and fights on their behalf. And the sooner this goal is achieved, the sooner our job will be done.[68]

The first round of elections had the opposite effect as the Sunnis, who felt they had been cut out of Iraq's future, boycotted the elections.[69]

As the minority in Iraq when compared with the Shiites, the Sunnis saw popular elections as a sure path to Shia dominance in the government.[70] Additionally, the Sunnis believed they would be called upon by the US-led coalition to form the post-Saddam government as they held the majority of people with government and administrative experience, and because a Shia-dominated Iraqi government would give Iran greater influence.[71] The Sunnis formed their own local governments to maintain order and to position themselves favorably for participation in the future national government,[72] but these bottom-up initiatives at governance were cast aside by Bremer,[73] further alienating Sunnis.

On 8 June 2004 the United Nations Security Council Resolution 1546 mandated a series of elections and votes to reach a democratically elected government in Iraq.[74] Key elements of the planned path to democracy included a vote in January 2005 to elect an interim National Assembly to draft the Iraqi constitution. The people of Iraq would vote to approve or reject the constitution in October of 2005. If accepted, then the next vote in December 2005 would select the first permanent democratic Iraqi government.[75]

Several other significant events unfolded in the latter half of 2004. The Coalition Provisional Authority returned sovereignty to Iraq under the Iraqi Interim Government on 28 June 2004, ending the occupation.[76] General George W. Casey Jr. assumed command of Multi-National Forces Iraq from Lieutenant General Sanchez the next month,[77] and conducted an assessment of the campaign in order to refine the strategy, determining that "Iraqi Army formation needed to be accelerated."[78] To this end, Lieutenant General David Petraeus, who commanded the 101st Air Assault Division during the invasion and first year of occupation, was assigned as the commander of the Multi-National Security Transition Command-Iraq (MNSTC-I) which had the task of training Iraqi Security Forces.[79] As Malkasian noted, "Petraeus returned to oversee the creation of 300,000 Iraqi security forces which included 120,000 men for 10 Iraqi Army divisions."[80]

Coalition and Iraqi forces conducted operations in Najaf, Baghdad, and Samarra to quell violent uprisings, but the second assault on Fallujah drew the most attention. Casey took the time to build political will and legitimacy for the offensive which was designed to rid the city of the 3,000-6,000 insurgents then controlling Fallujah. Once the Iraqi Interim Government gave its full support for the operation known as *AL FAJR*, the combined U.S. and Iraqi force commenced operations on 7 November 2004 and killed or captured 2,000 insurgents.[81]

Following up the offensive with reconstruction and governance initiatives and resources paid dividends in Fallujah. Indicative of the success of the operation – planned and resourced through all phases – was the 65 to 80 percent turnout of the population of Fallujah for three separate elections in 2005. After the combat ended, US and Iraqi security forces patrolled the city together to prevent the return of insurgents. As further evidence of the success of the operation, Malkasian observed, "When sectarian violence broke out in Baghdad in 2006, Sunnis fled to Fallujah because they considered it the safest city in Iraq."[82] Contributing to this perception of security was the presence of a police force raised by the Marines comprised of local Sunnis from Fallujah.[83] Although not officially the strategy at the time, Operation *AL FAJR* was a clear example of clear, hold, build.

Casey's campaign plan emphasized the fact that the coalition was battling an insurgency, not executing the final stages of the invasion plan. Additionally, Casey's plan acknowledged the shift from occupying power to one of supporting the Interim Iraqi Government. The wording of the plan was different from previous plans in that it replaced the terms "offensive operations" and "stability operations" with "full spectrum counterinsurgency operations."[84] Understanding the nature of the fight,[85] Casey was able to articulate a strategy that could produce meaningful gains toward defeating the insurgency, shepherding along the Iraqi political process, and eventually withdrawing US forces.

Recognizing the threat as an insurgency was only the beginning. According to Bing West, Casey had basically three options to choose from to deal with the insurgency: offensive operations to wipe out the insurgents; classic counterinsurgency operations using a clear and hold method; or "the third option: transition security responsibility to Iraqis. . . Casey chose the transition strategy. The main effort was to build the Iraqi forces."[86] Malkasian explained,

> The planners viewed the Iraqi Army as the lynchpin of effective counterinsurgency. From their perspective, the Iraqi Army could both provide vital manpower and gather intelligence better than coalition forces. Plus, Iraqi soldiers would not be perceived as occupiers, undercutting a major cause of the insurgency. It was thought that the Iraqi Army could eventually shoulder the burden of counterinsurgency operations, allowing the coalition to withdraw. Accordingly, Casey directed coalition forces to shift their focus from fighting insurgents to training Iraqis.[87]

What the planners perhaps missed was the fact that the Iraqi Army was often seen as a sectarian militia by those of the opposite sect of Islam. In the case of the Sunnis, the Iraqi Army, predominately Shia, was seen as predatory not protective. It would not be until local communities had the authority to raise forces to secure themselves that the sought after manpower, popular support, and intelligence would materialize.

In addition to the creation of MNSTC-I to take over training Iraqi Security Forces, Casey envisioned transition teams of 10-12 personnel each assigned at battalion through division level in every Iraqi Army formation.[88] This signaled a dramatic increase in advisory capacity, about 1,200 total, compared to the 350 advisors at the beginning of the campaign.[89] Coalition units also partnered with Iraqi units as a means of improving Iraqi forces' training and confidence. These were all steps taken in support of Casey's strategy of developing Iraqi forces to assume security responsibilities. The focus had shifted from killing insurgents to developing Iraqi Security Forces better suited to the task of securing Iraq from internal threats.[90]

Although development of the Iraqi security forces became the centerpiece to the US-led coalition strategy, the coalition and Iraqi military leaders were not operating in unison at the highest levels. The senior Iraqi military leadership's strategy was completely enemy-focused while the coalition strategy was more broad.[91] Describing the interaction between the Iraqi Ground Forces Command the and US-led Multi-National Corps-Iraq during the surge, a senior adviser to the Iraqi Ground forces Command noted, "Only in one short period of time did we ever bring the staffs together and develop a coherent plan together, and then it just kind of fell apart. It was a bit of a façade."[92]

Despite the perceived progress toward democracy on the political front (as Iraqis turned out to vote and all of the planned steps toward an Iraqi elected government were met), Iraq began to disintegrate into chaos as sectarian violence pushed the country into civil war, partly due to Sunni perceptions of continued disaffection[93] and partly due to insurgents fomenting sectarian attacks. Bing West marks the start of the civil war,

> On February 22 [2006], al Qaeda blew up the al-Askariya Golden Mosque in Samarra, a sacred Shiite shrine. With that sacrilege, the Jordanian-born terrorist Zarqawi succeeded in touching off the civil war he had murdered so many thousands to consummate. Urged on by Sadr, impassioned militiamen leaped into cars, vans, and minitrucks and sped out of Sadr City in east Baghdad to ransack Sunni neighborhoods and mosques. Both Sadr's Jesh al Mahdi and the Badr Corps militia launched attacks.[94]

In Baghdad, the coalition was unable to quell the violence or secure the population as up to 100 civilians died as a result of sectarian attacks per day.[95] Coalition forces conducted two major operations in Baghdad in attempts to regain control. These efforts failed, as acknowledged on 19 October by the coalition.[96] The unraveling of Iraqi society amid sectarian violence required another shift in strategy.[97] In fact, sectarian attacks increased significantly during the course of the coalition operations.[98]

The Sunnis in Al Anbar found themselves in a difficult position. The Iraqi security forces were predominately Shia because, believing the

Sunni insurgency would prevail, the Sunnis had refused to participate in the political process or to send their sons to join the army or police. As Malkasian observed, "many Sunnis refused to compromise, regardless of Coalition efforts to redress Sunni inequality, because they believed the insurgency would succeed militarily."[99] Although Sunnis had long rebuffed coalition efforts to gain Sunni support to stabilize Iraq, once the coalition and Iraqi government began to gain ground politically and militarily, Sunnis were forced to re-evaluate their position.[100]

As the traditional tribal leadership in Al Anbar was fractured,[101] third-tier sheiks led efforts to change course against the insurgency in the province, starting with the Albu Mahals and the Albu Nimr tribes in Al Qaim.[102] To oust the insurgents, these two tribes joined together and formed their own local militia called the Hamza battalion, which actively resisted Al Qaeda in Iraq. In response, the insurgents recruited two rival tribes and drove the Albu Mahals and Albu Nimr tribes from the city. Once the Marines finally drove the insurgents from the city, the Albu Mahals and Albu Nimr tribes regained their positions in the community and formed a large part of the Iraqi Army and police forces in the area while the tribesmen helped prevent the re-emergence of insurgents by assisting in providing local security.[103] While the tribal resistance to the insurgents in Al Qaim did not ignite the Al Anbar Awakening, Sheik Sittar, the leader of the Al Anbar Awakening gave credit for this mini-awakening to the Albu Mahals.[104]

The Al Anbar Awakening

The only bright spot in 2006 was the Al Anbar Awakening. Led by Shaykh Abd al Sittar Bezia Ftikhan al Rishawi who openly opposed Al Qaeda, this tribal movement shifted the balance in Al Anbar away from the extremist elements and toward cooperation with coalition forces to rid the province of the brutal insurgency.[105] Described by Najim Abed al Jabouri,

Partnering with the United States in 2006 was mainly an attempt to recoup Sunni losses once the United States had seemingly changed its position in their regard. This happened as the Sunni community increasingly saw al Qaeda and Iran as bigger threats than the U.S. occupation. . . The Anbar Awakening was an Iraqi grassroots initiative supported by the United States and paid for by the Iraqi government.[106]

While the decision and risk of the Awakening belonged to the Iraqis in Al Anbar, the movement was encouraged by coalition forces. As noted by Major Niel Smith and Colonel Sean MacFarland in their 2008 article, the Awakening

… was the result of a concerted plan executed by U.S. forces in Ramadi. Tactical victory became a strategic turning point when farsighted senior leaders, both Iraqi and American, replicated the Ramadi model throughout Anbar province, in Baghdad, and other parts of the country, dramatically changing the Iraq security situation in the process.[107]

These officers served in the 1st Brigade of the 1st Armored Division which originally deployed to Tal Afar to replace the 3d ACR, but later relocated to Ramadi, the capital of Al Anbar province in May of 2006.

Due to the large size and population of the city, the brigade lacked sufficient combat power to control the city even though it had five maneuver battalions.[108] The brigade leadership realized that Iraqi security forces would be required to pacify the city, but without the cooperation of the local leaders and the population any security would be fleeting: "We had to convince the tribal leaders to rejoin the fight against Al Qaeda."[109]

The brigade's plan involved several key objectives: isolation of the insurgents; deny the insurgents sanctuary; and build Iraqi security forces with emphasis on police.[110] Recognizing the support of the population as the center of gravity, and the local tribal leaders as the key to popular support,[111] the brigade took measures to protect the local leaders who were cooperative. This conformed to Galula's First Law regarding the importance of the support of the population which stated,

> What is the crux of the problem for the counterinsurgent? It is not how to clean an area. We have seen that he can always concentrate enough forces to do it, even if he has to take some risk in order to achieve the necessary concentration. The problem is, how to keep an area clean so that the counterinsurgent forces will be free to operate elsewhere. This can be achieved only with the support of the population.[112]

To protect the source of popular support, the brigade collaborated with the local leaders to form irregular security forces. In the words of Smith and MacFarland, "We established neighborhood watches that involved deputizing screened members of internal tribal militias as 'Provisional Auxiliary Iraqi Police,' authorizing them to wear uniforms, carry weapons, and provide security within the defined tribal area."[113]

In addition to creating irregular security forces, the brigade also changed its message to the local sheiks to convey resolve. As Smith and MacFarland wrote in their article, "Instead of telling them that we would leave soon and they must assume responsibility for their own security, we told them that we would stay as long as necessary to defeat the terrorists. That was the message they had been waiting to hear."[114] With the confidence that they would have an ally against the insurgents, the local leaders supported coalition efforts to recruit from the tribes to form additional irregular security forces as well as Iraqi Police. The popular support led by the sheiks allowed the nascent Sunni security forces to snuff out the insurgents in their tribal areas. As a former commander in

Ramadi commented, "The irregular security forces were really the key to success. When a tribal area would flip, all enemy activity in that area would stop overnight."[115] With the population firmly behind the Awakening, the security forces in Al Anbar grew rapidly, and effectively eradicated the insurgency there by April of 2007.[116]

The Surge

The final major shift in the strategy coincided with the arrival of General David Petraeus as the senior commander in Iraq, replacing Casey in February 2007. In addition to a new strategy, Petraeus arrived in Iraq amid the deployment of an additional five US Army brigade combat teams and two Marine infantry battalions. Malkasian observed, "Upon taking command on February 10, Petraeus incorporated the best lessons...into the security plan for Baghdad...Over 50 small outposts...manned by Iraqi police, the Iraqi Army, and US soldiers were emplaced throughout the city."[117] While the strategy became known as "the Surge" based on the surge of troops into theater, the deployment of additional forces was only a component of the plan. The new strategy focused on securing the population to create time and space for political reconciliation versus building Iraqi security forces.[118] General Petraeus communicated his vision for the clear-hold-build strategy on 19 March 2007, stating,

> Improving security for Iraq's population is … the over-riding objective of your strategy. Accomplishing this mission requires carrying out complex military operations and convincing the Iraqi people that we will not just "clear" their neighborhoods of the enemy, we will also stay and help "hold" the neighborhoods so that the "build" phase that many of their communities need can go forward.[119]

Unfortunately, as the emphasis was on the Iraqi Army, the Iraqi security forces fielded to this point were not well-suited to conduct the long-term hold phase.

Prior to the Surge, the US-led coalition lacked a viable strategy to establish security and stability in Iraq under Iraqi control, the prerequisites for withdrawal of US forces. In July of 2007, General Petraeus issued his Counterinsurgency Guidance which included the following: "Secure the people where they sleep, give the people justice; Every unit must advise their ISF partners; and, Include ISF in your operations at the lowest possible level."[120] Stated simply, the Iraqi and coalition forces had to secure the population to allow the political process to occur.

Despite the increase in coalition combat power and the application of a new strategy, without the support of the local populations the plan would fail. As Kitson advised, "… the political leadership should take precedence over the military because the ultimate aim is usually political, and the means of achieving it are also political in so far as they are concerned with gaining control of the population."[121] Galula made the point that the key objective in counterinsurgency is for the population:

> If the insurgent manages to dissociate the population from the counterinsurgent, to control it physically, to get its active support, he will win the war because, in the final analysis, the exercise of political power depends on the tacit or explicit agreement of the population or, at worst, on its submissiveness. Thus the battle for the population is a major characteristic of the revolutionary war.[122]

By the early stages of 2008 it was apparent that the Surge was working as violence was dramatically decreased after an initial uptick as increased numbers of security forces entered hotly contested areas.[123] David Ucko cites two main factors as the source of the success at this point: "First, the Sunni community was increasingly turning against the extremist – or *takfiri* – groups such as Al Qaeda in Iraq (AQI), creating a split in the Sunni-led insurgency. … The second factor behind the reduction in violence was the U.S. military's change in strategy."[124] Further, Ucko credits the US military with applying Galula's second law.[125] "By co-opting the middle ground and working with it against more extreme elements, the US military not only helped achieve common goals but also contributed to the marginalization of hardliners."[126]

As Ucko pointed out, the Al Anbar Awakening greatly contributed to the success of the Surge by fracturing the Sunni insurgency. Another way in which the Awakening impacted the Surge was the development of the Sons of Iraq program that sought to replicate the Sunni shift away from the insurgents beyond the confines of Al Anbar and across all of Iraq. As a former brigade commander in Baghdad commented regarding these irregular security forces, "I will tell you that they were probably the most critical piece, the greatest key to our success."[127] Najim Abed al Jabouri offered this description of the Sons of Iraq: "The Sons of Iraq program was a U.S.-led and -funded initiative to spread the success of the Anbar Awakening into other Sunni areas, particularly heterogeneous areas, and was not fully supported by the Iraqi government."[128]

The Sons of Iraq program initially sought to capitalize on the Sunni movement in Al Anbar to inspire other Sunnis across Iraq to resist the insurgents. The program eventually expanded to incorporate Shia Sons of Iraq groups. As James Corum noted,

> When a nation is faced with instability and disorder, there is an inevitable response for local citizens to establish militias and irregular forces for their own security. It is politically unwise, perhaps even impossible, for any national government to ignore the issue of local militias, which are based on the natural desire for local security.[129]

Some of the willing recruits for the Sons of Iraq were probably motivated only by the financial gain or increased status, but as Corum described above the natural desire to protect their families and communities was the dominant motivation. As a former brigade operations officer in Iraq commented regarding the Sons of Iraq, "Even though they were not well trained and did not have uniforms, their mere presence on the checkpoints was a psychological boost for the populace."[130]

Najim Abed al Jabouri's assessment also pointed to security as the primary reasons Iraqis were anxious to form their own Sons of Iraq groups, "Since tribes are cross-sectarian social organizations, news of the Anbari tribes defeating AQI traveled fast. Sunnis in other AQI-infested areas, such as in northern and western Baghdad, wanted the same type of access to the Americans as Sheikh Sattar."[131] One of the main differences in the motivations between members of the Awakening and the Sons of Iraq was the threat of sectarian violence. Many of the Sunnis who lived in Shia dominated areas wanted to raise Sons of Iraq groups to protect them from sectarian violence waged by Shia dominated security forces.[132]

Conclusions

Those responsible for planning and preparing for the invasion of Iraq in 2003 failed to develop, resource, and implement viable plans for operations after the conventional combat phase concluded. The US exit strategy assumed that post-conflict operations would be brief and quickly turned over to Iraqis. Tom Ricks described a background interview Jay Garner conducted regarding the post combat phase:

> Among the principles he laid down for the postwar Iraq was that an obtrusive U.S. role would be short and the Iraqi army would continue to exist. "We intend to immediately start turning some things over, and every day, we'll turn over more things," Garner said. … The overall duration of the U.S. presence, he said, would be short. "I'll probably come back to hate this answer, but I'm talking months."[133]

Due in part to a superficial understanding of Iraq's complex society and internal dynamics, the failure to plan and the assumption that the campaign would be brief resulted in poor strategy. The strategy shifts and lack of familiarity with previous counterinsurgency campaigns was disruptive to efforts to raise security forces.

These failures were compounded by the Bush administration's denial of the insurgency in its early stages.[134] Galula pointed out that in the cold revolutionary war phase, when the insurgents are largely operating within the law, it is difficult to justify a response to the insurgent threat.[135]

Similarly, Sir Robert Thompson wrote, ". . .during the build-up phase [of an insurgency], the signs are not always recognized, and the existence of a subversive movement may even be ignored or denied for short-sighted political reasons."[136] But the US-led coalition had just toppled the government (hardly a cold phase in any regard) and the actions of the insurgents were not difficult to recognize as violent threats inconsistent with Galula's cold phase. Were attacks on coalition forces the acts of final hold-outs hopelessly resisting the US-led occupation or something else?

As mentioned previously, Iraqi security forces (mainly army) were the key to the US exit strategy. Iraqi security forces would solve the problem of growing violence, and by allowing US forces to leave, would remove the source of agitation and restore a sense of nationalism. Recall Lieutenant General Conway's comment in 2004: "The situation will change when Iraqi Army divisions arrive. They will engender people with a sense of nationalism. Together with an elected government, they will create Stability."[137]

There was no such thing as Iraqi nationalism in post-Saddam Iraq. Because the US neglected to develop an understanding of Iraqi society in order to formulate viable plans for the post-combat phase, those in charge of developing the New Iraqi Army did not understand the impact of sectarian friction on the effectiveness of any Iraqi military operation.[138] Najim Abed al Jabouri summed up the friction succinctly:

> Misunderstanding between the United States and Iraqi Sunni Arabs fed the insurgency. When coalition forces invaded Iraq in March 2003, the predominantly Sunni provinces of Anbar, Ninevah, and Salah al-Din did not want to confront the invading forces militarily. ... The reigning U.S. assumption at the time was that the political vacuum created by the fall of the former regime would strengthen the position of the tribal leaders. . . Meanwhile, Sunnis—in particular those without deep ties to the former regime—assumed that the United States would broker with them, since Sunnis had more government experience than any of the other ethnic or sectarian groups. Sunnis also assumed it was not in the U.S. interest to give the majority of the next government to Shia and Kurdish opposition groups, most of which were connected to Iran.[139]

These failures directly impacted the US strategy to secure Iraq after the fall of Saddam's regime. As Tony Cordesman wrote in his assessment of Iraqi Security Forces, "The United States did more than fail to plan for an effective effort to secure the country or to develop effective Iraqi forces before or during the invasion. It failed to deal with the risk – and then with the reality – of a growing insurgency effort for nearly a year after the fall of Saddam Hussein."[140] The inability (or unwillingness) to acknowledge the nature of the campaign limited the US-led coalition's ability to develop an appropriate response.

General Abizaid took command of CENTCOM in July of 2003 and diagnosed the violence in Iraq as "a classical guerrilla-type campaign."[141] Recognition of the threat as a guerrilla or insurgent campaign apparently had little impact on strategy. A brief scan of even the table of contents of the works of classic counterinsurgency theorists would have led to many of the basic principles for successful counterinsurgency campaigns discussed thus far. For example, the table of contents of Sir Robert Thompson's work, *Defeating Communist Insurgency, The Lessons of Malaya and Vietnam*, lists "Basic Principles of Counter-Insurgency" as beginning on page 50.[142] Among these principles, Thompson advises the counterinsurgent to "secure its base areas first," advising that "priority in respect of security measures should be given to the more highly developed areas of the country" as they contain the majority of the population.[143]

Eventually, US strategy focused on securing the population versus destroying the insurgents. Recall General Petraeus' vision as the senior commander in Iraq which stated, "Improving security for Iraq's population is…the over-riding objective of your strategy."[144] In pursuit of this vision, Petraeus required additional troops to expand security to a greater part of the population. The simple increase of US forces may have worked on its own, but when combined with a new strategy focused on securing the population which isolated the insurgents from bases of support, places to hide, and pools from which to recruit, the addition of combat forces contributed to success.

The most important factor which contributed to success was the shift in the support of the population sparked by the Al Anbar Awakening. As a retired general officer of the British Army commented, "An army can defeat an army. An army can't defeat a people."[145] To paraphrase, the Iraqi Army cannot defeat an insurgency, only the Iraqi people can. As each of the counterinsurgency theorists discussed advised, counterinsurgency is a political struggle with victory going to the side which gains the support of the population.

Sending more coalition troops was not a viable consideration at any rate based on political repercussions and strained resources. Additional coalition forces would not likely have swayed the population to stand against the insurgents, or to provide additional intelligence. According to Najim Abed al Jabouri,

> Surge troops that came to Anbar in 2007 were not seen as useful, other than on the eastern border with Baghdad where the ISF acted as a sectarian militia. In fact, U.S. troops in general were not seen as useful even before the surge. … Sheikh Sattar told the Americans … the U.S. forces could stay on their bases

while the Anbaris fought, since they knew who the al Qaeda fighters were.[146]

Nor would greater numbers of often sectarian Iraqi Army battalions have caused the population to throw their support behind the central government as neither side, Sunni and Shia, trusted the other.

The difference in the Al Anbar Awakening, and later the Sons of Iraq, was the ability of the population to take matters into their own hands to secure themselves and their interests. As Najim noted,

> Contrary to a growing U.S. narrative about the Sunni Awakening being mainly the fruit of U.S. counterinsurgency tactics, in Ramadi having the U.S. forces in the neighborhoods was not what made the people feel safe. They felt safe when their men could join the police force and secure their areas by themselves.[147]

It is important to re-emphasize Najim's point above. The Surge alone did not turn things around in Iraq. The shift in the dialogue between coalition forces and disaffected Sunnis bolstered the change in strategy to focus on securing the population.

The irregular security forces in the Iraq campaign represented many things to the various sides of the conflict. To the Iraqi government and the US-led coalition, they represented a shift in popular support away from the insurgents. The insurgents and their supporters undoubtedly saw the Al Anbar Awakening and the Sons of Iraq as the greatest threat to their ability to operate in Iraq. To the people, the families and neighbors of the Sons of Iraq, they were trustworthy protectors with common interests. A retired British Army general advised, "If the terrorists come from the people, you're not going to defeat the people, and therefore you've got to influence the terrorists in such a way that they will stop fighting."[148] Once the people turned against the insurgents, the insurgents had no chance of success.

Notes

1.   For an explantion of the origins of the Al Anbar Awakening and the Sons of Iraq and their differences, see Najim Abed Al-Jabouri and Sterling Jensen, "The Iraqi and AQI Roles in the Sunni Awakening," PRISM, Vol. 2 Issue No. 1, National Defense University Press, Washington, D.C., December 2010.

2.   Michael R. Gordon and General Bernard E. Trainor, *Cobra II: the Inside Story of the Invasion and Occupation of Iraq*, (New York: Vintage Books, February 2007), 13. "A no-fly zone was decreed over northern Iraq, effectively making Kurdistan an autonomous enclave. Six months later, as the Iraqis kept up their air raids against the Shiites, a no-fly zone was belatedly established over southern Iraq as well."

3.   Gordon and Trainor, *Cobra II*, 13. "The Bush administration settled on a policy of economic sanctions, military containment, and regular United Nations inspections to dismantle Saddam's programs to develop nuclear, biological, and chemical weapons. It was a strategy for a slow, steady squeeze, not deeper involvement."

4.   Gordon and Trainor, *Cobra II*, 14.

5.   Gordon and Trainor, *Cobra II*, 29. "When it came to Iraq, Franks was not starting with a blank slate. General Binford Peay, the commander of the 101st Airborne during the Gulf War, had been appointed to run CENTCOM in 1994. He had been particularly concerned about a 'Basra breakout,' the possibility that Saddam would mass five divisions in the southern part of Iraq and rush them into Kuwait before the Americans could respond. If war came, the United States would defend Saudi Arabia, again fight to reclaim Kuwait, and then press north into Iraq."

6.   Gordon and Trainor, *Cobra II*, 31.

7.   General Tommy Franks, *American Soldier*, (New York: Harper Collins, 2004), 182. General Franks assumed command of Third Army in May of 1997.

8.   Gordon and Trainor, *Cobra II*, 29. "Containing Saddam was not the problem. It was filling a potential power vacuum that worried him."

9.   Franks, *American Soldier*, 182, 198. General Franks assumed command of Third Army in May of 1997, and CENTCOM in July 2000.

10. Franks, *American Soldier*, 315. Relating a conversation with Secretary Rumsfeld: "Mr. Secretary," I said, "we have a plan, of course. OPLAN 1003." "What's your opinion of it, General?" "Desert Storm II. It's out of date, under revision because conditions have changed. We have different force levels in the region than we had when the plan was written. And we obviously have learned some valuable lessons about precision weapons and Special Operations from our experience in Afghanistan."

11. Franks, *American Soldier*, 385.

12. Gordon and Trainor, *Cobra II*, 28-29. "Franks later described the constant back and forth between them as an 'iterative process.' Gingrich had a more apt description: it was 'constant negotiation.'"

13.   Gordon and Trainor, *Cobra II,* 4. "Greg Newbold, the three-star general who served as chief operations deputy for the JCS, had the main assignment for the session. He was to outline Central Command's OPLAN 1003-98, the military's contingency plan in the event of a war with Iraq. ... As Newbold outlined the plan, which called for as many as 500,000 troops, it was clear that Rumsfeld was growing increasingly irritated. ... Myers asked Rumsfeld how many troops he thought might be needed. The defense secretary said in exasperation that he did not see why more than 125,000 troops would be required and even that was probably too many."

14.   The United Nations Security Council issued resolutions against Iraq following the Iraqi invasion of Kuwait, and the US-led coalition's ouster of Saddam Hussein's forces from Kuwait in 1991. For an in-depth account of the 1991 war in the Persian Gulf, see *Certain Victory* by Brigadier General Robert M. Scales, published by Brassey's in 1997.

15.   Dr. Donald P. Wright and Colonel Timothy R. Reese, *On Point II: Transition to the New Campaign*, (Kansas: Combat Studies Institute Press, August 2008), 10-11.

16.   Colonel Gregory Fontenot, US Army, Retired; Lieutenant Colonel E.J. Degen, US Army; Lieutenant Colonel David Tohn, US Army, *On Point*, (Kansas: Combat Studies Institute Press, 2004), 86.

17.   Wright and Reese, *On Point II*, 622.

18.   Franks, *American Soldier*, 428. "Ground troops" refers to Army and Marine forces and does not indicate combat troops, but rather includes support troops as well. "By the third week of March, our total strength in all components — including our Gulf State Coalition allies in Kuwait — would number 292,000. Of these, there would be approximately 170,000 soldiers and Marines assigned to the Combined Forces Land Component Command (CFLCC)."

19.   BB010, Battalion Commander. Interview by Mark Battjes and Nathan Springer, 2 March 2011.

20.   Franks, *American Soldier*, 339-341. Referring to the diagram on page 340, "The starbursts at the intersections of Lines and Slices represented points of focus we would use to develop the specifics of a detailed plan. For example, the starburst at the intersection of 'Operational Fires' and 'Leadership' meant we would attack leadership targets using bombs and missiles. Simply stated, the starbursts helped the Component Commanders and staff match specific military tools to specific targets, resulting in better synergy among traditionally independent arms and services."

21.   Franks, *American Soldier*, 423. "Over the weeks ahead, Jay Garner and I would meet; he would build a team of specialists and experts from across the U.S. government, deploy the team to Kuwait, establish links with our commanders on the ground, and prepare to enter Iraq on the heels of our attacking troops. . . Secured by Coalition forces, these teams would work with Iraqis to build local governance in each major population center. And local Iraqis would represent every ethnic, tribal, and religious interest in the country in establishing national leadership."

22.   Franks, *American Soldier*, 424.

23. Bing West, *The Strongest Tribe: War, Politics, and the Endgame in Iraq,* (New York: Random House, 2008), 5.

24. Franks, *American Soldier*, 421. "... Congress passed, and President Clinton signed, the Iraq Liberation Act of 1998. This legislation declared that it would be the "policy of the United States to seek to remove the Saddam Hussein regime from power in Iraq and to replace it with a democratic government." The Act directed the President to designate one or more suitable Iraqi opposition organizations to receive assistance."

25. Nadia Schadlow, "War and the Art of Governance," *Parameters* (Autumn 2003): 85.

26. Franks, *American Soldier*, 419.

27. Gordon and Trainor, *Cobra II*, 165.

28. Schadlow, "War and the Art of Governance," 88. "Civilian leaders supported the Army's leadership over governance operations largely because of a lack of alternatives. Political leaders realized that the Army was the only agency capable of accomplishing reconstruction in the midst of and aftermath of combat. While some World War II leaders expressed concern that civilians could 'lose' the postwar world by default (by failing to offer a 'comprehensive plan to rival that of the Army's'), President Roosevelt recognized that only the Army would be able to deliver 'prompt results.' Even the Secretary of State, James Byrnes, acknowledged that the State Department did not have the capacity to run an occupation."

29. West, *The Strongest Tribe*, 6.

30. West, *The Strongest Tribe*, 5-6. "Saddam's reign of terror had ended, but chaos was about to reign. Throughout the city, American commanders stood off to one side as mobs rushed like locusts into hundreds of government buildings and stripped them clean. ... I asked an American colonel what he was going to do to restore order. 'Nothing,' he said. 'I have no such orders. They deserve whatever they can haul away, after what Saddam did to them.' In early May, Ambassador Zalmay Khalilzad and Assistant Secretary of State Ryan C. Crocker visited Baghdad and left shocked by the chaos and the American paralysis. Washington responded not by addressing the systemic failures of a detached military and a rudderless administration, but by replacing Garner."

31. Gordon and Trainor, *Cobra II*, 533.

32. Wright and Reese, *On Point II*, 23.

33. Wright and Reese, *On Point II*, 26. "Ambassador Bremer arrived with the Bush administration's charge to dramatically reshape Iraq, a mandate which led to two major decisions. ... On 16 May Bremer issued CPA Order No. 1, 'De-Baathification of Iraqi Society,' which removed from public life those Iraqis who had held the top four ranks in the Baath Party and subjected to review members with lesser ranks. ... CPA Order No. 2, 'Dissolution of Entities,' quickly followed on 23 May and disbanded all of Saddam's military and intelligence institutions, rendering hundreds of thousands of Iraqi soldiers jobless."

34. Wright and Reese, *On Point II*, 26.

35. Franks, *American Soldier*, 393.

36. Wright and Reese, *On Point II*, 26-27. "Many Coalition military figures believed at the time that these important CPA decisions created a pool of disaffected and unemployed Sunni Arabs from which a growing insurgency could later recruit."

37. Najim Abed Al-Jabouri and Sterling Jensen, "The Iraqi and AQI Roles in the Sunni Awakening," *PRISM*, Vol. 2 Issue No. 1, National Defense University Press, Washington, D.C., December 2010, 5.

38. West, *The Strongest Tribe*, 10.

39. West, *The Strongest Tribe*, 10.

40. West, *The Strongest Tribe*, 11-12.

41. Carter Malkasian, "Counterinsurgency in Iraq," Counterinsurgency in Modern Warfare. Daniel Marston and Carter Malkasian (eds.), (Oxford: Osprey Publishing, 2010), 290.

42. David Galula, *Counterinsurgency Warfare Theory and Practice*, (New Dehli: Praeger Security International, 2010), 60.

43. Galula, *Counterinsurgency Warfare Theory and Practice*, 59. "The division of the over-all action into successive steps following each other in logical order facilitates the tactical tasks of the agents; they know at each step what the intermediate objectives is and what they have to do to reach it."

44. Galula, *Counterinsurgency Warfare Theory and Practice*, 59.

45. West, *The Strongest Tribe*, 23. For example, "Maj. Gen. Charles H. Swannack, commanding the 82nd, told the sheiks that he wasn't going to tolerate the attacks against his paratroopers, which had increased from twelve a day in October to twenty a day in November. The JTF initiated Operation Iron Hammer, a get tough (or tougher) approach to quelling the insurgency. Attack aircraft with thousand-pound bombs were directed at insurgent hideouts and arms caches, the wives of insurgents were detained for questioning, and uncooperative villages were sealed off with barbed wire."

46. West, *The Strongest Tribe*, 30.

47. West, *The Strongest Tribe*, 30.

48. Malkasian, "Counterinsurgency in Iraq," 291. "The ensuing offensive ignited widespread Sunni outrage. Viewing it as an attack on their society, Sunnis poured into Fallujah from other Sunni cities. When the Marines stepped off, they encountered heavy resistance from roughly 2,000 insurgents."

49. Wright and Reese, *On Point II*, 626.

50. Malkasian, "Counterinsurgency in Iraq," 291-292. Because of the increase in violence in southern Iraq, the British also pushed for an end to the offensive in Fallujah.

51. This implies that prior to the first assault on Fallujah there was a strategy. As discussed previously, Jay Garner, who was supposed to execute the post-combat phase of the campaign, was replaced after only three weeks on the ground. If there was a strategy it may have left with Garner. Lieutenant General Sanchez and L. Paul Bremer apparently had no strategy to cope with the aftermath of the

fall of Saddam's regime or the growing insurgency.

52. Secretary of State Condoleezza Rice, Opening Remarks before the Senate Foreign Relations Committee, 19 October 2005, http://www.globalsecurity.org/military/library/congress/2005_hr/051019-rice.pdf, (accessed 19 May 2011), 1-4. "In 2003, enforcing UN resolutions, we overthrew a brutal dictator and liberated a nation. Our strategy emphasized the military defeat of the regime's forces and creation of a temporary government with the Coalition Provisional Authority and an Iraqi Governing Council. In 2004, President Bush outlined a five step plan to end the occupation: transferring sovereignty to an Iraqi interim government, rebuilding Iraq's infrastructure, getting more international support, preparing for Iraq's first national election this past January, and helping establish security. ... In 2005, we emphasized transition: a security transition to greater reliance on Iraqi forces and a political transition to a permanent, constitutional democracy. ... Now we are preparing for 2006. ... We are moving from a stage of transition toward the strategy to prepare a permanent Iraqi government for a decisive victory. ... With our Iraqi allies, we are working to: *Clear* the toughest places — no sanctuaries to the enemy — and disrupt foreign support for the insurgents. *Hold* and steadily enlarge the secure areas, integrating political and economic outreach with our military operations. *Build* truly *national* institutions working with more capable provincial and local authorities. ... None of these elements can be achieved by military action alone. None are purely civilian. All require an integrated civil-military partnership."

53. Galula, *Counterinsurgency Warfare Theory and Practice*, 4.

54. See the first chapter for a brief discussion of some of the prominent counterinsurgency theorists and authors.

55. West, *The Strongest Tribe*, 9.

56. Wright and Reese, *On Point II*, 166-167.

57. Malkasian, "Counterinsurgency in Iraq," 293.

58. Wright and Reese, *On Point II*, 166.

59. Malkasian, "Counterinsurgency in Iraq," 293.

60. Malkasian, "Counterinsurgency in Iraq," 293. "Success in developing the Iraqi Nation Guard and other forces depended entirely on the attitudes of the local population. National Guard battalions based on the Kurdish militia (*peshmerga*), or Shi'a militias, performed adequately. Battalions based on Sunnis did not. Disaffected from the Iraqi government and angry at the coalition, at this stage in the war, Sunnis generally sympathized with the insurgency and had no intention of fighting their fellow tribesmen or family members."

61. Malkasian, "Counterinsurgency in Iraq," 293. "There is little doubt that the US military could have done a better job advising and training the Iraqis. Few commanders embedded advisers with local forces. Yet at this time, even when Americans did, Sunnis remained reluctant to fight."

62. Franks, *American Soldier*, 393.

63. Malkasian, "Counterinsurgency in Iraq," 294.

64. West, *The Strongest Tribe*, 74. "Petraeus had agreed to train on a priority

basis 1,000 former soldiers from the Habbaniyah area. But the Sunni recruits refused to leave the province, or fight alongside Americans and have their own people turn against them."

65. Wright and Reese, *On Point II*, 449. As an example, referring to the 2d Battalion of the New Iraqi Army, "Sunni soldier in the unit refused to engage in combat against Sunni insurgents. ..."

66. West, *The Strongest Tribe*, 74. "The Shiite battalions stationed near Baghdad didn't want to come to Anbar and be shot at."

67. West, *The Strongest Tribe*, 39.

68. President George W. Bush, National Address, Carlisle PA, 24 May 2004, (accessed 31 May 2011), http://georgewbush-whitehouse.archives.gov/news/ releases/ 2004/05/print/20040524-10.html

69. West, *The Strongest Tribe*, 41.

70. Najim and Jensen, "The Iraqi and AQI Roles in the Sunni Awakening," 8. "However, the announcement of the Interim Governing Council in July 2003, 5 months after the invasion, confirmed Sunni suspicions that the United States intended to de-Sunnify Iraq and tilt the regional balance of power toward Iran. Choosing Shia and Kurdish opposition groups close to Iran to form the next Iraqi government not only was a catalyst for national resistance, but it also created the conditions for the national resistance — now being led by once-skeptical former military and Ba'athist officials — to tolerate, trust, and in some instances embrace jihadists and al Qaeda as means to spoil American objectives. After the interim government had formed, the majority of Sunnis, rather than just the margins, significantly distrusted U.S. intentions. Ideas circulated through the Sunni community that the United States was changing its alliances in the Middle East because it now considered Shia religious extremism less threatening to its long-term interests in the region than Sunni religious extremism, especially the Wahhabism coming from Saudi Arabia. Whether the United States intended to de-Sunnify Iraq and change the regional balance of power from Sunni to Shia leadership did not matter at this point. Sunnis were now convinced this was the case."

71. Najim and Jensen, "The Iraqi and AQI Roles in the Sunni Awakening," 4. "Misunderstanding between the United States and Iraqi Sunni Arabs fed the insurgency. When coalition forces invaded Iraq in March 2003, the predominantly Sunni provinces of Anbar, Ninevah, and Salah al-Din did not want to confront the invading forces militarily. As Sunnis in the north saw the destruction and looting taking place in the south as coalition troops entered, a number of tribal leaders who had been in contact with U.S. military and intelligence personnel prior to the invasion convinced the Iraqi military and Ba'ath party leadership in Anbar, Ninevah, and Salah al-Din to meet with the Americans upon their arrival. The reigning U.S. assumption at the time was that the political vacuum created by the fall of the former regime would strengthen the position of the tribal leaders. Therefore, brokering with the tribes was a means to communicate with civil-military leaders and in turn to influence the populace. Meanwhile, Sunnis — in particular those without deep ties to the former regime — assumed that the United States would broker with them, since Sunnis had more government experience than any of the other ethnic or sectarian groups. Sunnis also assumed it was not in

the U.S. interest to give the majority of the next government to Shia and Kurdish opposition groups, most of which were connected to Iran. Giving the Shia and Kurds responsibility for the government would increase Iranian influence in Iraq."

72. Najim and Jensen, "The Iraqi and AQI Roles in the Sunni Awakening," 5. "In the early days of the post-invasion, the tribes convinced military and political leaders in Anbar, Ninevah, and Salah al-Din to negotiate an arrangement until the next government took shape. Military and Ba'ath party leaders were chosen as interim governors and police chiefs through temporary elections in Ninevah and through appointment by tribal leaders in Anbar and Salah al-Din. The Sunni leaders in these provinces thought that doing so would spare their cities and personal property and would put them in leadership positions for the next government."

73. West, *The Strongest Tribe*, 14. "… word went out over the classified military Internet — Bremer will decide when, where, and how any election will be held. … The military stood down their plan for local elections."

74. Wright and Reese, *On Point II*, 627.

75. West, *The Strongest Tribe*, 39.

76. Wright and Reese, *On Point II*, 627.

77. Wright and Reese, *On Point II*, 627.

78. Malkasian, "Counterinsurgency in Iraq," 296. "In 2004 Casey conducted a review of the campaign and determined, with advice from COIN expert Kalev Sepp, that Iraqi Army formation needed to be accelerated."

79. Wright and Reese, *On Point II*, 176. "The new organization, Multi-National Security Transition Command-Iraq (MNSTC-I), would follow the newer vision for the ISF. Major General Petraeus, who commanded the 101st AABN during the invasion of Iraq in March 2003, was selected and promoted to be the first three-star commander of MNSTC-I, taking command on 6 June 2004."

80. Malkasian, "Counterinsurgency in Iraq," 294.

81. Malkasian, "Counterinsurgency in Iraq," 295-296.

82. Malkasian, "Counterinsurgency in Iraq," 296.

83. Correspondence with a Marine adviser in Iraq in 2004 to 2005.

84. Wright and Reese, *On Point II*, 177.

85. Carl von Clausewitz, *On War*, ed. and trans. Michael Howard and Peter Paret (Princeton, NJ: Princeton University Press, 1976), 88–9. "As the first, the supreme, the most far reaching act of judgment that the statesman and commander have to make is to establish the kind of war on which they are embarking, neither mistaking it for, nor trying to turn it into something that is alien to its nature. This is the first of all strategic questions and the most comprehensive."

86. West, *The Strongest Tribe*, 70-71.

87. Malkasian, "Counterinsurgency in Iraq," 297.

88. Malkasian, "Counterinsurgency in Iraq," 297.

89. Wright and Reese, *On Point II*, 456.

90. Malkasian, "Counterinsurgency in Iraq," 297. "From their perspective, the Iraqi Army could both provide vital manpower and gather intelligence better than coalition forces. Plus, Iraqi soldiers would not be perceived as occupiers, undercutting a major cause of the insurgency."

91. BC010, Field Grade Officer. Interview by Robert Green and Aaron Kaufman, 1 March 2011.

92. BC010, Field Grade Officer. Interview by Robert Green and Aaron Kaufman, 1 March 2011

93. Carter Malkasian, "The Role of Perceptions and Political reform in Counterinsurgency: The Case of Western Iraq, 2004-2005." *Small Wars and Insurgencies*, Vol. 17, no 3, September 2006, pp. 370-371.

94. West, *The Strongest Tribe*, 114-115.

95. Malkasian, "Counterinsurgency in Iraq," 302.

96. Malkasian, "Counterinsurgency in Iraq," 302. "On October 19, Major General William Caldwell, the coalition spokesman, acknowledged that Operation *Together Forward II* had failed."

97. Malkasian, "Counterinsurgency in Iraq," 304. "The civil war forced a major change in US strategy. The Republican defeat in the midterm elections, followed by the Iraq Study Group report, made it impossible for Bush to ignore the deteriorating situation. The Iraq Study Group. ... recommended placing greater effort in expanding and training the Iraqi security forces, particularly the Iraqi Army. The group also called for benchmarks to measure the progress of the Iraqi government toward political reconciliation, and negotiating with Iraq's neighboring countries."

98. Lieutenant General Michael D. Maples, US Army, Director, Defense Intelligence Agency, "The Current Situation in Iraq and Afghanistan, Statement for the Record Senate Armed Services Committee," (15 November 2006), 3. http://www.fas.org/irp/congress/ 2006_hr/111506maples.pdf, (accessed 20 May 2011),"Overall attacks averaged approximately 180 per day in October 2006, up from approximately 170 the previous month, and 70 in January 2006. Daily average of attacks against Iraqi Security Forces in October more than doubled the number reported in January, approximately 30 compared to 13. Daily average of attacks on civilians in October was four times higher than reported in January, approximately 40 compared to 10."

99. Carter Malkasian, "The Role of Perceptions and Political reform in Counterinsurgency: The Case of Western Iraq, 2004-2005," *Small Wars and Insurgencies*, Vol. 17, no 3, September 2006, pp. 367-368.

100. Malkasian, "The Role of Perceptions and Political reform in Counterinsurgency," p. 368. "When the Coalition and Iraqi Interim Government broke this perception through a series of military and political successes, Sunnis made serious approaches to find a compromise."

101. Najim and Jensen, "The Iraqi and AQI Roles in the Sunni Awakening," 12. "The Iraqi Islamic Party (IIP) controlled the Anbar Provincial Council, and al Qaeda's murder and intimidation campaign and word of a U.S. armored brigade (1–1 AD) coming to Ramadi in spring 2006 to conduct a large, Fallujah-like

military sweep of the city sent the provincial and municipal council into exile. The tribal leadership was also in exile, leaving mainly third-tier tribal leaders in the province."

102.   James   A.   Russell,   *Innovation,   Transformation,   and   War: Counterinsurgency Operations in Anbar and Ninewa Provinces, Iraq, 2005 to 2007,* (Stanford University Press, Stanford, CA, 2011) 60.

103.   Russell, *Innovation, Transformation, and War*, 60-61.

104 .   BH040, Afghanistan Veterans Panel. Interview by Richard Johnson, Aaron Kaufman, Nathan Springer, and Thomas Walton, 24 March 2011.

105.   Malkasian, "Counterinsurgency in Iraq," 304.

106.   Najim and Jensen, "The Iraqi and AQI Roles in the Sunni Awakening," 4.

107.   Major Niel Smith and Colonel Sean MacFarland, "Anbar Awakens: the Tipping Point," *Military Review* (March-April 2008): 41.

108   Smith and MacFarland, "Anbar Awakens: the Tipping Point," 43. These battalions included Marine and Army units.

109.   Smith and MacFarland, "Anbar Awakens: the Tipping Point," 43. As an aside, the article also describes the previous attempt by Sunni leaders in Al Anbar to oust the insurgents while simultaneously battling the coalition forces, which failed.

110.   Smith and MacFarland, "Anbar Awakens: the Tipping Point," 43.

111. See David Galula, *Counterinsurgency Warfare Theory and Practice*, p. 53. Discussion of the active minority: "The Second Law: Support Is Gained Through an Active Minority. The original problem becomes now: how to obtain the support of the population — support not only in the form of sympathy and approval but also in active participation in the fight against the insurgent. The answer lies in the following proposition, which simply expresses the basic tenet of the exercise of political power: In any situation, whatever the cause, there will be an active minority for the cause, a neutral majority, and an active minority against the cause. The technique of power consists in relying on the favorable minority in order to rally the neutral majority and to neutralize or eliminate the hostile minority."

112.   Galula, *Counterinsurgency Warfare Theory and Practice*, 52.

113.   Smith and MacFarland, "Anbar Awakens: the Tipping Point," 43.

114.   Smith and MacFarland, "Anbar Awakens: the Tipping Point," 44.

115.   BA010, Brigade Commander. Interview by Richard Johnson and Thomas Walton, 22 February 2011. "We got the Iraqi government to pay them. Now they are taking the government's salt, and they're swearing allegiance to the government of Iraq. They weren't a tribal militia with no affiliation to the ISF. They were an adjunct to the ISF. They were an extension of them. ... I used them mostly in the neighborhood watch mode which allowed me to use the actual IPs proper into the city and into the more problematic areas. . . The irregular security forces were really the key to success. When a tribal are...would flip, boom, all enemy activity in that area would stop overnight. ... The important thing was

they were providing their own security. ... They knew exactly who the bad guys were in those areas and they were able to let them know, 'Hey the bottom rail's on top now; either clean up your act or get out of town' ... Were some of these guys former insurgents? Absolutely. I'm sure they were. ... But I didn't care. All that mattered to me was my soldiers and marines weren't being killed anymore in those areas. That's what mattered to me."

116. Malkasian, "Counterinsurgency in Iraq," 304. "Sittar's movement backed local police forces. Because they were Sunni, the local community would give the police intelligence, enabling them to kill or detain more insurgents than the Iraqi Army. The number of police actively in operations grew from fewer than 1,000 in early 2006 to over 7,000 in early 2007. By April, the police had managed to suppress insurgent activity in Ramadi, and most of the key tribes of Al Anbar had aligned with Sittar's movement."

117. Malkasian, "Counterinsurgency in Iraq," 304.

118. Malkasian, "Counterinsurgency in Iraq," 304. "His top priority was protecting the people rather than building the Iraqi Army (although that remained a critical task). In his view, the point of the surge was to create a breathing space in the violence...in which political reconciliation could take place."

119. General David Petraeus, Note to Troops, Baghdad, 19 March 2007.

120. General David Petraeus, MNF-I COIN Guidance, Baghdad, July 2007.

121. Kitson, *Low Intensity Operations,* 41.

122. Galula, *Counterinsurgency Warfare Theory and Practice*, 4. "Afflicted with his congenital weakness, the insurgent would be foolish if he mustered whatever forces were available to him and attacked his opponent in a conventional fashion, taking as his objective the destruction of the enemy's forces and the conquest of the territory. Logic forces him instead to carry the fight to a different ground where he has a better chance to balance the physical odds against him. The population represents this new ground."

123. Malkasian, "Counterinsurgency in Iraq," 305. "Violence escalated initially as US and Iraqi forces (ISF) moved into contested neighborhoods to create and man the joint security stations. ... In June 2007, at the height of the surge, there were more than 1,500 security incidents throughout Iraq; in August 2008, these had dropped to just under 200."

124. David Ucko, *The New Counterinsurgency Era: Transforming the US Military for Modern Wars,* (Washington DC: Georgetown University Press, 2009), 126. "The transition from larger isolated bases to smaller joint security stations helped U.S. troops provide security, which enabled bridges to be built with local communities seeking greater stability or protection. ... In short, U.S. brigades moved from a narrow and predominantly enemy-centered focus on rooting out the insurgency to a broader effort to "end the cycle of violence," primarily by engaging with its adversaries' initial motivation to take up arms."

125. Galula, *Counterinsurgency Warfare Theory and Practice*, 53. "The Second Law: Support Is Gained Through an Active Minority. The original problem becomes now: how to obtain the support of the population — support not only in the form of sympathy and approval but also in active participation

in the fight against the insurgent. The answer lies in the following proposition, which simply expresses the basic tenet of the exercise of political power: In any situation, whatever the cause, there will be an active minority for the cause, a neutral majority, and an active minority against the cause. The technique of power consists in relying on the favorable minority in order to rally the neutral majority and to neutralize or eliminate the hostile minority."

126. Ucko, *The New Counterinsurgency Era*, 126.

127. BE060, Brigade Commander. Interview by Mark Battjes and Thomas Walton, 9 March 2011.

128. Najim and Jensen, "The Iraqi and AQI Roles in the Sunni Awakening," 3.

129. James Corum, *Training Indigenous Forces in Counterinsurgency: A Tale of Two Insurgencies*. http://www. strategicstudiesinstitute.army.mil/pubs/display.cfm?PubID=648 (accessed 13 March 2011): 48.

130. BG070, Field Grade Officer. Interview by Nathan Springer and Thomas Walton, 15 March 2011.

131. Najim and Jensen, "The Iraqi and AQI Roles in the Sunni Awakening," 13-15. "In the Anbar Awakening, Sunnis did not see benefit in having the U.S. combat forces stationed in the cities taking the lead in security operations. Sunnis felt the best way to combat AQI was through local security force recruitment and permission to conduct their own operations with support from the American troops. This was because Anbar is largely a homogeneous province in which Sunnis saw a U.S. troop presence in the cities as a clear sign of occupation. All efforts were made by Awakening leaders to distance themselves from being seen as supporting a U.S. occupation. For them it was ideal if the Iraqis could take the lead, with the United States playing a supporting role. This way they could show the populace that the Americans were their guests helping them fight the real occupiers, al Qaeda and Iran."

132. Najim and Jensen, "The Iraqi and AQI Roles in the Sunni Awakening," 13-14. "Abdul Sattar's Sunni visitors were generally from the mixed cities in Salah al-Din, Diyala, and Baghdad, where the Iraqi Police were already well established but were heavily sectarian. The Americans in these mixed areas were less likely to work with former insurgents or people who did not fully support the local ISF or government — Americans were inclined to only support local military and political leaders, even if those leaders lacked legitimacy or were seen as sectarian. In these heterogeneous areas, the Iraqi Police were often an instrument for sectarian violence where Sunnis sought a means to defend themselves legally."

133. Thomas E. Ricks, *Fiasco, The American Military Adventure in Iraq*, (New York: Penguin Group USA, 2007), 104.

134. West, *The Strongest Tribe*, 10. Secretary Rumsfeld did not see an insurgency growing in Iraq and explained away the growing violence as the work of "dead-enders."

135. Galula, *Counterinsurgency Warfare Theory and Practice*, 43-44. "The situation at this stage is characterized by the fact that the insurgent operates largely on the legal side, and only partly on the fringe of legality, through his

subversion tactics. He may or may not have been recognized as an insurgent; if he has been identified as such, only the police and a few people in the government generally realize what is looming. The essential problem for the counterinsurgent stems from the fact that the actual danger will always appear to the nation as out of proportion to the demands made by an adequate response. The potential danger is enormous, but how to prove it on the basis of available, objective facts? How to justify the efforts and sacrifices needed to smother the incipient insurgency?"

136. Sir Robert Thompson, *Defeating Communist Insurgency: The Lessons of Malaya and Vietnam* (New York: Frederick Praeger, 1967), 50.

137. Malkasian, "Counterinsurgency in Iraq," 294.

138. Had the administration worked through basic questions such as "Who is going to gain power?; Who is capable of administration at the national, provincial, and local levels?; Who is going to keep the lights on and the water running?" they might have identified some of the complexity of the Iraqi society.

139. Najim and Jensen, "The Iraqi and AQI Roles in the Sunni Awakening," 4. "Misunderstanding between the United States and Iraqi Sunni Arabs fed the insurgency. When coalition forces invaded Iraq in March 2003, the predominantly Sunni provinces of Anbar, Ninevah, and Salah al-Din did not want to confront the invading forces militarily. As Sunnis in the north saw the destruction and looting taking place in the south as coalition troops entered, a number of tribal leaders who had been in contact with U.S. military and intelligence personnel prior to the invasion convinced the Iraqi military and Ba'ath party leadership in Anbar, Ninevah, and Salah al-Din to meet with the Americans upon their arrival. The reigning U.S. assumption at the time was that the political vacuum created by the fall of the former regime would strengthen the position of the tribal leaders. Therefore, brokering with the tribes was a means to communicate with civil-military leaders and in turn to influence the populace. Meanwhile, Sunnis — in particular those without deep ties to the former regime — assumed that the United States would broker with them, since Sunnis had more government experience than any of the other ethnic or sectarian groups. Sunnis also assumed it was not in the U.S. interest to give the majority of the next government to Shia and Kurdish opposition groups, most of which were connected to Iran. Giving the Shia and Kurds responsibility for the government would increase Iranian influence in Iraq."

140. Anthony H. Cordesman, *Iraqi Security Forces, A Strategy for Success,* (Connecticut: Praeger Security International, 2006), p. 15.

141. West, *The Strongest Tribe*, 10.

142. Thompson, *Defeating Communist Insurgency*, 111.

143. Thompson, *Defeating Communist Insurgency*, 57.

144. General David Petraeus, Note to Troops, Baghdad, 19 March 2007.

145. BL070, Retired General Officer, Interview by Mark Battjes, Ben Boardman, Robert Green, Richard Johnson, Aaron Kauffman, Dustin Mitchell, Nathan Springer, and Thomas Walton, 30 March 2011.

146. Najim and Jensen, "The Iraqi and AQI Roles in the Sunni Awakening," 15.

147. Najim and Jensen, "The Iraqi and AQI Roles in the Sunni Awakening," 11. "Contrary to a growing U.S. narrative about the Sunni Awakening being mainly the fruit of U.S. counterinsurgency tactics, in Ramadi having the U.S. forces in the neighborhoods was not what made the people feel safe. They felt safe when their men could join the police force and secure their areas by themselves. Joining the police and working in their own local areas were also a way to avoid being targeted by the Americans. As policemen, they might have wanted U.S. support doing operations, but they did not want to support U.S. operations — as experienced by the Fallujah Brigade in 2004. Also, as policemen they received official pay and had better chances of winning reconstruction work in their areas."

148. BL070. Retired General Officer, 30 March 2011.

Chapter 5
Conclusions

Irregular security forces have had major impacts on the outcome of many counterinsurgency campaigns (e.g. *firqa*,[1] Sons of Iraq,[2] Philippine Constabulary). Irregular security forces are indigenous forces, not part of the regular police or military organizations of the host nation, that are recruited locally to provide a basic level of security in a given area. Irregular security forces, when used in conjunction with all other available capabilities, contribute to, but do not in and of themselves ensure success. As Major General Tony Jeapes concluded, "The *firqats'* understanding of ground and their speed of manoeuvre were both superior to SAF troops', but when it came to straight military tactics, the SAF's discipline told every time. The two forces were complementary; neither could have won the war alone."[3]

In Dhofar, the *firqa* added critical elements to the Sultan's campaign such as knowledge of local terrain,[4] the ability to convince other insurgents to switch sides,[5] and by securing cleared areas, the *firqa* enabled the Sultan's conventional forces to concentrate for offensive operations elsewhere. As John Akehurst described it in his book *We Won a War,*

> The *Firqats* at that time were about 1,400 strong and were the key to the centre and east. Considerable strength would be needed to take on the enemy in the west and it could only be amassed at the expense of the centre and east. Either the enemy must be cleaned out altogether, an impossible task in the short term, or the securing must be taken over by the *Firqats*.

The *firqa* relied heavily on conventional forces and capabilities to include their SAS advisers, fire support, logistics support, communications, and medical treatment. The regular and irregular forces in Dhofar formed a more complete fighting force complementing for the weakness of the other, and capitalizing on their respective strengths.

Due to their intimate knowledge of their local areas, the irregular security forces of the Awakening and the Sons of Iraq were able establish security where coalition and Iraqi Security Forces could not. According to a former commander in Ramadi during the Awakening, "The irregular security forces were really the key to success. When a tribal area would flip, all enemy activity in that area would stop overnight."[6] Each constituted forces capable of preventing the re-emergence of insurgents in cleared areas, and signaled a shift away from the insurgents toward the government. Each force relied to varying degrees on support from conventional forces and the Iraqi government which helped solidify their shift away from the insurgents.[7]

Paraphrasing Clausewitz,[8] counterinsurgents must understand the nature and the aim of the conflict in which they are engaged. Regarding irregular security forces, counterinsurgents must consider several factors to include the intended purpose of the force, how the force fits into the overall strategy, the nature and capabilities of the threat the irregular force will encounter, and the appropriate composition of the force to support the strategy and counter the threat.[9] Additional factors include the perception of legitimacy of the force in the eyes of the population, the type and duration of the training required, the location of employment, of the force, and the availability and competency of likely leadership for the force. Finally, counterinsurgents must be prepared to provide competent partnership and advisory support to the force in quantities sufficient to account for the size and distribution, or scope, of the irregular force. When raised with consideration of these aspects, irregular security forces provide additional capabilities to the host nation's efforts that conventional forces do not possess.

While irregular security forces could provide a multitude of capabilities to complement conventional forces, counterinsurgents must understand the purpose of such forces in the context of the overall strategy. When asked about the key aspects of raising irregular security forces, a former counterinsurgency practitioner and retired general officer from the British Army identified the purpose as the first requirement: "What is the aim? What are you trying to do? … Your aim must obviously be compatible with the government's aim, although they may not necessarily be exactly the same. They must be compatible. You must know what you're trying to do."[10]

When counterinsurgents recruit irregular security forces from, and employ them within, their local area, these forces prove useful in gathering intelligence, holding cleared areas, strengthening ties between the population and the government, and enabling other forces to focus on offensive operations against insurgents. Dependent upon the nature of the conflict and the myriad variables of the environment in which the campaign unfolds, irregular security forces could conduct surveillance tasks, fixed site security,[11] population control measures,[12] or augment regular forces during limited offensive operations. The purpose of the irregular security force within the greater context of the overall strategy drives the determination of the other requirements (i.e. training, equipping, advisory).

Counterinsurgents have used various strategies in previous campaigns. The French campaign in Algeria generated the *quadrillage*[13] strategy, whereas the US experience in Vietnam brought about the oil-spot strategy.[14] In Dhofar, Lieutenant Colonel John Watts devised the Five Fronts to guide SAS support to the Sultan's campaign.[15] The US strategy in Iraq shifted several times but eventually evolved into Clear, Hold, Build.[16] Counterinsurgents must have a clear strategy in order to raise proper irregular security forces which support the efforts of the host nation government to achieve its desired end state. As a retired British general officer observed, "A short-term success that doesn't affect the long-term aim is a failure."[17]

Counterinsurgents tend to overlook irregular security forces as a component of their strategy, instead focusing initially on increasing the capacities of army or police.[18] This indicates that either the observations of previous counterinsurgency practitioners have not been considered,[19] or the host nation has failed to identify the true nature of the conflict. Considering the primacy of the political in counterinsurgency operations,[20] and the supreme importance of popular support, properly raised irregular security forces are often more effective than other security forces in gaining the support of the population.

In counterinsurgency operations, irregular security forces serve as a symbol of popular support.[21] For this reason, counterinsurgents must understand the capabilities of the insurgents to avoid employing irregular forces beyond their capabilities. As FM 3-24 advises, counterinsurgents must employ irregular security forces in limited roles initially to build confidence and avoid politically costly defeat.[22]

It is important to understand the cultural and social factors that could potentially impact the effectiveness of an irregular security force. For example, in Dhofar, to avoid in-fighting and disintegration, *firqa* units were developed along tribal lines versus mixed tribal *firqa*.[23] As an SAS veteran of the Dhofar campaign observed, "It was only the first *firqa* that was a composite tribal mix. And then I think people realized pretty quickly that they needed a tribal based *firqa*."[24] Based on the discussion of sectarian violence in Iraq during Operation Iraqi Freedom,[25] the negative outcome of a mixed Sunni and Shia irregular security force are obvious.

In addition to the social considerations regarding the composition of irregular security forces, there are organizational considerations. Irregular security forces generally conduct operations within their local areas and therefore do not require a great deal of infrastructure or logistic support. Being light and agile is one of the advantages of irregular security forces. As an SAS veteran of Dhofar described the *firqa*:

> I suppose you would class them as light recce troops really.... They always travelled light. They rarely carried any weight. ... Most of them were pretty athletic. They were fast over the sort of first three to five meters, so in a contact they would move very quickly, but they couldn't carry weight for any distance. . . What we would often do is have a patrol at night, establish a position, before first light put up a light sangar, and then we'd get the helicopters to come in, and the first load would always bring in the mortar and a number of rounds.[26]

Should the host nation provide irregular security forces equipment such as vehicles, advanced communication systems, or heavy weapons, the host nation must also provide training and logistic support to the irregular force.

Irregular security forces provide the population a means to secure their own areas, and often, a source of income with which to support their families. Because one of the key benefits of irregular security forces is greater access and connection to the population which produces intelligence, the population must see irregular security forces as legitimate. Without the popular perception of legitimacy, irregular security forces will become disconnected from the population and lose their ability to operate effectively. As Ian Gardiner recounted regarding the benefit of the *firqa's* connection to the local population,

> As our former enemies they knew the ground and the tactics of their former friends intimately, and they were good at things that we were poor at, namely reconnaissance, gathering intelligence and communicating with the nomadic population. They were of that population after all. They were, therefore, extremely useful in retaining the peace in an area which had been cleared of *adoo*, thereby leaving conventional forces to get on with prosecuting the war elsewhere. For all their limitations, I do not believe we could have won the war without the *Firqat*.[27]

In order to create effective irregular security forces which suit their intended purpose as part of the overall strategy, counterinsurgents must have an understanding of the local population from which they are recruiting. Important factors which impact training include literacy, fluency in the local language and other dialects, social structures which may affect discipline, previous military or police experience, and health.[28] Counterinsurgents should train irregular security forces to maximize their natural capabilities. Recall T. E. Lawrence's advice: "Do not try to do too much with your own hands. Better the Arabs do it tolerably than that you do it perfectly. It is their war, and you are to help them, not to win it for them."[29] Members of the BATT in Dhofar offered the following advice: "The most important factor in selecting an irregular indigenous force is to establish their true motive for fighting and to use this as a bait as much as possible. In this way a force will be created using its own motivation which will hold it together and keep it going in difficult times."[30] This is especially true of those selected as leaders of irregular security forces as discussed later in this chapter.

Where irregular security forces operate is of critical importance. When irregular security forces operate on their own turf and they have the support of population, they gain several advantages over the insurgents. In this case, irregular security forces have intimate knowledge of the terrain and the population, and can access intelligence from the population which can provide early warning of attacks. By operating close to home, irregular security forces' logistics requirements are lessened. Additionally, because the local population sees their own family members providing for their security, they feel more secure, and are naturally more supportive.[31]

By their nature, irregular security forces generally do not have a pool of experienced veterans from which to select their leadership. There may be members of the community with prior experience in either the military or the police which can be beneficial. The most important aspect for irregular security force leadership is the support they enjoy from the local population and the members of the force. As a retired British general officer advised regarding leaders of irregular security forces: "There's got to be somebody who is a leader, in local terms, not necessarily someone who meets our staff college requirements. He's got to be a local leader. He's got to be respected. He's got to have a following otherwise there's no point in having him."[32]

As David Galula stated, "[T]he turning point really comes when leaders have emerged from the population and have committed themselves on the side of the counterinsurgent. They can be counted upon because they have proved their loyalty in deeds and not in words, and because they have everything to lose from a return of the insurgents."[33] In the case of the Sons of Iraq, the key leadership was at the tribal sheik level. Once these sheiks made the decision to take coalition support against the insurgents, the population by and large followed their lead.[34] In Dhofar, the *firqa* generally chose their own leaders, but when operating with a BATT, the SAS man commanding the BATT was essentially the *firqa* commander as well.[35] The question of leadership must be answered by the local population and approached by the counterinsurgents as a matter of compromise versus confrontation.[36] What works for them? If they don't accept the leader, his qualifications to lead are irrelevant.

Partnering irregular security forces and conventional forces provides many benefits. By partnering conventional and irregular forces, each has access to the other's unique capabilities (e.g. knowledge of local terrain, access to fire support).[37] Each force is able to learn from the other during training and operations. Partnership between irregular and conventional forces can also mitigate the negative effects of poor irregular force leadership by developing those leaders over time.[38]

Although similar to partnership, embedding advisers into irregular force units instead makes the adviser part of the team. Advisers share hardships and burdens, provide a constant source of advice, expertise, and leadership, and access to conventional force capabilities.[39] The CSAF in 1972 summed up the effect of competent advisers, "*Firqats* supported by 22 SAS should achieve a lot: *Firqats* supported by a small party from SAF or unsupported will achieve little. They might even decamp to the Coastal Plain."[40]

Not all good soldiers make good advisers. Given the importance of the advisory mission, and the above criteria for effective advisors, counterinsurgents must regard selection of officers for advisory duty as a positive and beneficial assignment, selecting only those best qualified. As Ian Gardiner wrote, "Regular soldiers could find the *Firqat* infuriating. The SAS, who themselves were somewhat irregular, and were trained to train irregular soldiers, were mostly pretty well adjusted to the task."[41]

Critical to the success of advisory missions are advisers that can speak the language of the forces with which they are operating. One former SAS adviser to the *firqa* in Dhofar identified the lack of language capability as the greatest source of friction between the *firqa* and their advisers.[42] As a retired British officer who commanded SAS troops in Dhofar related, "My directive stated that my primary task was to train surrendered enemy personnel."[43] This task was made easier by the language capabilities within his command. "18 of my soldiers, out 65, could speak Arabic. Every four man patrol had an Arabist."[44]

The final key aspect is scope. How many irregular security forces are needed in how many areas by when to achieve the purpose in support of the strategy? If only a small number of such forces are needed in only a few areas, the host nation may perhaps be able to apply more resources and time to develop them. Should the scope of the requirement for irregular security forces be great, counterinsurgents should avoid rapidly raising large numbers of forces with little training or leadership.[45]

All of the aspects discussed above are interconnected. Changes in one ripples into changes in all. The first aspect counterinsurgents must address is the purpose in the context of the strategy. What does the host nation hope to achieve by raising irregular security forces? If that is not understood, the other aspects cannot be accurately factored into the development of appropriate irregular security forces.

While this thesis does not cover the topic of irregular security forces in counterinsurgency with sufficient depth to be used as a sole source for raising such forces, it is a starting point. Within each of the aspects discussed there are multiple variables which counterinsurgents must identify and consider as they develop plans to raise irregular security forces. For example, what impact does simple and affordable communications devices have on the ability of less experienced indigenous leaders to command and control irregular security forces and access support from other forces?

Much remains to be learned regarding irregular security forces. Additional case studies of other campaigns would expand the body of knowledge on this topic. Intelligence services may have some lessons to share regarding irregular security forces, but those lessons would most likely push the research and the thesis into classified areas. Perhaps one of the yet untapped sources for further study of irregular security forces is

Soviet material from the era of cold war and proxy wars.

Irregular security forces have proven to be a powerful capability in counterinsurgency operations. They have never been the silver bullet or associated counter to insurgency. Irregular security forces provide capabilities which are different than, but complementary to, conventional forces, and should be considered as a component of any counterinsurgency operation.

Notes

1. See Chapter Three for a detailed discussion of the *firqa* in Oman.

2. See Chapter Four for a detailed discussion of the Sons of Iraq.

3. Tony Jeapes, *SAS: Secret War,* (Surrey: Harper Collins, 1996), 237.

4. John Akehurst, *We Won a War: The Campaign in Oman 1965-1977* (Great Britain: Biddles Ltd.), 43. "I must reiterate how vitally important the *Firqats* were in the struggle. Their knowledge of the ground and their influence with the civilians were indispensible, and worth all the time, trouble and money spent to secure and retain their goodwill and allegiance."

5. BL070, Retired General Officer. Interview by Mark Battjes, Ben Boardman, Robert Green, Richard Johnson, Aaron Kaufman, Dustin Mitchell, Nathan Springer, and Thomas Walton, 30 March 2011. Cites Salim Mubarak as saying, "We are going to form a *firqa* of all the people coming down [from the Jebel to join the Sultan]…and then we will sweep them [*adoo*] off the Jebel!"

6. BA010, Brigade Commander. Interview by Richard Johnson and Thomas Walton, 22 February 2011. "We got the Iraqi government to pay them. Now they are taking the government's salt, and they're swearing allegiance to the government of Iraq. They weren't a tribal militia with no affiliation to the ISF. They were an adjunct to the ISF. They were an extension of them. … I used them mostly in the neighborhood watch mode which allowed me to use the actual IPs proper into the city and into the more problematic areas. … The irregular security forces were really the key to success. When a tribal area would flip, boom, all enemy activity in that area would stop overnight. … The important thing was they were providing their own security. … They knew exactly who the bad guys were in those areas and they were able to let them know, 'Hey the bottom rail's on top now; either clean up your act or get out of town'. … Were some of these guys former insurgents? Absolutely. I'm sure they were. … But I didn't care. All that mattered to me was my soldiers and marines weren't being killed anymore in those areas. That's what mattered to me."

7. For a detailed discussion of the differences between the Al Anbar Awakening and the Sons of Iraq, see Najim Abed Al-Jabouri and Sterling Jensen, "The Iraqi and AQI Roles in the Sunni Awakening," *PRISM*, Vol. 2 Issue No. 1, National Defense University Press, Washington, D.C., December 2010, p. 4.

8. Carl von Clausewitz, *On War*, ed. And trans. Michael Howard and Peter paret (Princeton, N.J.: Princeton University Press, 1976), 88–9. "As the first, the

supreme, the most far reaching act of judgment that the statesman and commander have to make is to establish the kind of war on which they are embarking, neither mistaking it for, nor trying to turn it into something that is alien to its nature. This is the first of all strategic questions and the most comprehensive."

9.   See Chapter Two for a detailed discussion of the key aspects to consider for irregular security force development.

10.   BL070, Retired General Officer, 30 March 2011.

11.   Fixed security points include traffic control points (both vehicular and foot traffic), securing critical infrastructure, and other static guard duties.

12.   Population control measures include census taking, controlling access to secured population centers, curfew enforcement, rationing commodities, and searching persons, dwellings, and vehicles for contraband.

13.   For a complete discussion of the French strategy in Algeria, see David Galula, Counterinsurgency Warfare Theory and Practice, *Pacification in Algeria 1956-1958*. Santa Monica: RAND, 2006, pp. 5-25 and 243-270, and Roger Trinquier, *Modern Warfare: A French View of Counterinsurgency*. Ft Leavenworth: CSI, 1985, pp. 67-93.

14.   Robert Komer, *Bureaucracy at War, U.S. Performance in the Vietnam Conflict* (Boulder, CO: Westview Press, 1986), 135. Assistant Secretary Roger Hilsman's final memorandum to the Secretary of State in March 1964 called for "primary emphasis on giving security to the villagers. The tactics are the so-called oil-blot approach, starting with a secure area and extending it slowly. ... This calls for the use of military forces in a different way from that of orthodox, conventional war. Rather than chasing Viet Cong, the military must put primary emphasis on clear-and-hold operations and on rapid reinforcement of villages under attack. It is also important of course, to keep the Viet Cong regular units off balance by conventional offensive operations, but these should be secondary to the major task of extending security..."

15.   Jeapes, *SAS: Operation Oman*, 31.

16.   National Security Council, "National Strategy for Victory in Iraq," The White House, 30 November 2005, available at: http://www.whitehouse.gov/infocus/iraq/iraq_national_strategy_20051130.pdf, p. 8. "Objective: To develop the Iraqis' capacity to secure their country while carrying out a campaign to defeat the terrorists and neutralize the insurgency. To achieve this objective, we are helping the Iraqi government: *Clear* areas of enemy control by remaining on the offensive, killing and capturing enemy fighters and denying them safe-haven, *Hold* areas freed from enemy control by ensuring that they remain under the control of a peaceful Iraqi government with an adequate Iraqi security force presence, *Build* Iraqi Security Forces and the capacity of local institutions to deliver services, advance the rule of law, and nurture civil society."

17.   BL070, Retired General Officer, 30 March 2011.

18.   As examples, in Malaya the initial response to the crisis was to rapidly expand the police force in short order whereas in Iraq and Afghanistan the initial emphasis was placed on building armies to improve security.

19.   For more detail on the principles developed by various counterinsurgency

practitioners and scholars, see Chapter One of this thesis.

20.   David Galula, *Counterinsurgency Warfare Theory and Practice*, (Florida: Hailer, 2005), 89. "That the political power is the undisputed boss is a matter of both principle and practicality. What is at stake is the country's political regime, and to defend it is a political affair. Even if this requires military action, the action is constantly directed toward a political goal. Essential though it is, the military action is secondary to the political one, its primary purpose being to afford the political power enough freedom to work safely with the population."

21.   Galula, *Counterinsurgency Warfare Theory and Practice*, 57. "When troops live among the population and give it protection until the population is able to protect itself with a minimum of outside support, the insurgent's power cannot easily be rebuilt, and this in itself is no mean achievement. But the turning point really comes when leaders have emerged from the population and have committed themselves on the side of the counterinsurgent. They can be counted upon because they have proved their loyalty in deeds and not in words, and because they have everything to lose from a return of the insurgents."

22.   FM 3-24, 6-16. "Committing poorly trained and badly led forces results in high casualties and invites tactical defeats. While defeat in a small operation may have little strategic consequence in a conventional war, even a small tactical defeat of HN forces can have serious strategic consequences in a COIN. Insurgent warfare is largely about perceptions. Effective insurgent leaders can quickly turn minor wins into major propaganda victories. Defeat of one government force can quickly degrade the morale of others. If a HN force fails, the local populace may begin to lose confidence in the government's ability to protect them."

23.   Tribal alignment was a lesson learned and an example of a successful adaptation on the part of the SAS in Dhofar after the first mixed tribe *firqa* collapsed after the death of its leader, Salim Mubarak.

24.   BL330, Interview by Robert Green with SAS Dhofar veteran, UK, 28 March 2011

25.   See Chapter Four.

26.   BL330, Interview with SAS Dhofar veteran.

27.   Ian Gardiner, *In the Service of the Sultan: A First Hand Account of the Dhofar Insurgency*. (South Yorkshire, England: Pen & Sword Books Unlimited, 2007), 159

28.   BATT Notes on Raising and Training of Irregular Forces in Dhofar, Annex B to Section 10 of unknown report, Middle East Centre, St. Anthony's College, Oxford, UK, 1. Recruits that were too old, too young, or in very sick were rejected as unfit for the rigors of combat.

29.   Lieutenant Colonel T.E. Lawrence, "Twenty-Seven Articles," *The Arab Bulletin*, Article No. 8, 27 August 1917. While Lawrence referred directly to Arabs as that was his experience, the same advice is probably valuable when raising irregular security forces in any country or among any ethnic group.

30.   BATT Notes, 1.

31.   Najim and Jensen, "The Iraqi and AQI Roles in the Sunni Awakening," 11.

32.   BI080, Retired General Officer. Interview by Ben Boardman, Robert Green, Nathan Springer, and Thomas Walton, 3 April 2011.

33.   Galula, Counterinsurgency Warfare Theory and Practice, Praeger, 57.

34.   Najim and Jensen, "The Iraqi and AQI Roles in the Sunni Awakening," 11. "After Abdul Sattar had announced the Anbar Awakening, working with the Americans was a means of securing Sunni areas."

35.   BL330, Interview with SAS Dhofar veteran, UK, 28 March 2011. "You had a firqa leader, an Arab firqa leader who was from the tribe but when BATT was with the firqa it was the BATT commander who was the firqa leader. So when I was with the firqa I was the firqa leader, and that was true of all the BATT/firqa relationships. So you were actually in command, and what you said was an order even though perhaps there was some negotiation before you would go firm on that. The BATT commander was in charge of the group shall we say, the firqa. That maybe puts a slightly different perspective on it."

36.   BL330, Interview with SAS Dhofar veteran, UK, 28 March 2011. "It was the way you chose to lead the firqa whether it was successful or not, whether you were in constant confrontation or you compromised and achieved an operational objective."

37.   Najim and Jensen, "The Iraqi and AQI Roles in the Sunni Awakening," 15.

38.   General Stanley McCrystal, "COMISAF Initial Assessment (UNCLASSIFIED)," (Kabul, Afghanistan: Headquarters International Security Assistance Force, 30 August 2009), G-2

39.   Peter Chiarelli and Patrick Michaelis, "The Requirements for Full-Spectrum Operations." *Military Review*, 85:4 (July-August 2005): 7-8. "Over 500,000 hours of dedicated training by an embedded advisory staff, who lived, ate, and trained with the Iraqi Army, resulted in over 3,000 Iraqi missions executed independent of coalition presence in and around Baghdad. This critical step in the progress toward establishing full independence was accomplished through a robust advisory system where the division embedded over 70 full-time military advisory teams per Iraqi battalion over the course of the deployment. Resourced down to the platoon level, the advisors leveraged the cultural importance of relationships to the Arab people to build trust and rapport and create momentum toward a truly professional military force."

40.   CSAF Assessment, 11.

41.   Gardiner, *In the Service of the Sultan*, 156.

42.   BI330, Dhofar Veteran. Interview by Robert Green, 28 March 2011. "But coming back to the importance of language, perhaps; that was a major problem that was never fully acknowledged I do think. A lot of the guys just did not understand what the guy was saying, and then tempers would get frayed and people would get very heated when there was no need to do so."

43.   BI090, Retired General Officer. Interview by Ben Boardman, Robert Green, Nathan Springer, and Thomas Walton, 4 April 2011.

44.   BI090, Retired General Officer. Interview by Ben Boardman, Robert

Green, Nathan Springer, and Thomas Walton, 4 April 2011.

45.   FM 3-24, 6-16. "Committing poorly trained and badly led forces results in high casualties and invites tactical defeats. While defeat in a small operation may have little strategic consequence in a conventional war, even a small tactical defeat of HN forces can have serious strategic consequences in a COIN. Insurgent warfare is largely about perceptions. Effective insurgent leaders can quickly turn minor wins into major propaganda victories. Defeat of one government force can quickly degrade the morale of others. If a HN force fails, the local populace may begin to lose confidence in the government's ability to protect them."

Bibliography
Primary Sources

Interviews

Command and General Staff College (CGSC) Scholars Program 2011. Scholars Program *Counterinsurgency Research Study 2011*. Research Study, Fort Leavenworth, KS: Ike Skelton Chair in Counterinsurgency, 2011. This study included oral history interviews of counterinsurgency practitioners and policy professionals from the United States and United Kingdom. All interviews are held with the Ike Skelton Chair in Counterinsurgency, CGSC Fort Leavenworth, KS.

Boston, Massachusetts

BF020, Civilian Adviser to MNF-I. Interview by Richard Johnson and Aaron Kaufman, 11 March 2011.

Fort Bliss, Texas

BB010, Battalion Commander. Interview by Mark Battjes and Nathan Springer, 2 March 2011.

BB020, Battalion Commander. Interview by Mark Battjes and Nathan Springer, 2 March 2011.

BB030, Brigade Commander. Interview by Mark Battjes and Nathan Springer, 3 March 2011.

Fort Bragg, North Carolina

BC010, Field Grade Officer. Interview by Robert Green and Aaron Kaufman, 1 March 2011.

BC020, Brigade Commander. Interview by Robert Green and Aaron Kaufman, 2 March 2011.

BC030, Battalion Commander. Interview by Benjamin Boardman and Richard Johnson, 1 March 2011.

BC040, Battalion Commander. Interview by Benjamin Boardman and Richard Johnson, 2 March 2011.

BC050, Battalion Commander. Interview by Benjamin Boardman and Richard Johnson, 2 March 2011.

BC060, Battalion Commander. Interview by Benjamin Boardman and Richard Johnson, 3 March 2011.

Fort Irwin, California

BE010, Transition Team Leader. Interview by Mark Battjes and Thomas Walton, 7 March 2011.

BE020, Transition Team Member. Interview by Mark Battjes and Thomas Walton, 7 March 2011.

BE030, Company Commander. Interview by Mark Battjes and Thomas Walton, 8 March 2011.

BE040, Transition Team Leader. Interview by Mark Battjes and Thomas Walton, 9 March 2011.

BE050, Battery Commander. Interview by Robert Green and Aaron Kaufman, 8

March 2011.

BE060, Brigade Commander. Interview by Mark Battjes and Thomas Walton, 9 March 2011.

BE070, Field Grade Officer. Interview by Robert Green and Aaron Kaufman, 9 March 2011.

BE080, Battalion Commander. Interview by Robert Green and Aaron Kaufman, 7 March 2011.

BE090, Battalion Commander. Interview by Robert Green and Aaron Kaufman, 7 March 2011.

Fort Knox, Kentucky

BD010, Field Grade Officer. Interview by Benjamin Boardman and Dustin Mitchell, 14 March 2011.

BD020, Commander. Interview by Benjamin Boardman and Dustin Mitchell, 14 March 2011.

BD030, Commander. Interview by Benjamin Boardman and Dustin Mitchell, 14 March 2011.

BD040, Commander. Interview by Benjamin Boardman and Dustin Mitchell, 15 March 2011.

BD050, Commander. Interview by Benjamin Boardman and Dustin Mitchell, 15 March 2011.

BD060, Field Grade Officer. Interview by Benjamin Boardman and Dustin Mitchell, 16 March 2011.

BD070, Field Grade Officer. Interview by Benjamin Boardman and Dustin Mitchell, 16 March 2011.

BD080, Field Grade Officer. Interview by Benjamin Boardman and Dustin Mitchell, 17 March 2011.

Fort Leavenworth, Kansas

BA010, Brigade Commander. Interview by Richard Johnson and Thomas Walton, 22 February 2011.

BA020, Battalion Commander. Interview by Mark Battjes and Benjamin Boardman, 23 February 2011.

BA030, Vietnam Veteran. Interview by Aaron Kaufman and Dustin Mitchell, 24 February 2011.

BA040, Brigade Commander. Interview by Aaron Kaufman and Dustin Mitchell, 23 February 2011.

BA050, Battalion Commander. Interview by Robert Green and Nathan Springer, 23 February 2011.

BA060, Battalion Commander. Interview by Robert Green and Nathan Springer, 23 February 2011.

BA070, Battery Commander. Interview by Richard Johnson and Thomas Walton, 24 February 2011.

BA080, Counterinsurgency Adviser. Interview by Richard Johnson and Nathan Springer, 9 March 2011.

BA090, Brigade Commander. Interview by Mark Battjes and Benjamin Boardman, 24 February 2011.

Fort Stewart, Georgia

BG010, Battalion Commander. Interview by Nathan Springer, 14 March 2011.

BG020, Brigade Commander. Interview by Mark Battjes and Thomas Walton, 14 March 2011.

BG030, Troop Commander. Interview by Mark Battjes, Nathan Springer, and Thomas Walton, 14 March 2011.

BG040, Brigade Commander. Interview by Nathan Springer and Thomas Walton, 15 March 2011.

BG050, Battalion Commander. Interview by Mark Battjes, 15 March 2011.

BG060, Battalion Commander. Interview by Mark Battjes, 15 March 2011.

BG070, Field Grade Officer. Interview by Nathan Springer and Thomas Walton, 15 March 2011.

BG080, Battalion Commander. Interview by Mark Battjes and Thomas Walton, 16 March 2011.

BG090, Battalion Commander. Interview by Mark Battjes and Nathan Springer, 16 March 2011.

BG100, Brigade Commander. Interview by Mark Battjes and Nathan Springer, 16 March 2011.

United Kingdom

BI010, Senior British Officer. Interview by Mark Battjes, Benjamin Boardman, Robert Green, Richard Johnson, Aaron Kaufman, Dustin Mitchell, and Nathan Springer, 29 March 2011.

BI020, Battle Group Commander. Interview by Aaron Kaufman and Thomas Walton, 31 March 2011.

BI030, Field Grade Officer. Interview by Robert Green and Thomas Walton, 29 March 2011.

BI040, Field Grade Officer. Interview by Mark Battjes and Dustin Mitchell, 1 April 2011.

BI050, Dhofar Veterans Panel. Interview by Mark Battjes, Ben Boardman, Robert Green, Richard Johnson, Aaron Kaufman, Dustin Mitchell, Nathan Springer, and Thomas Walton, 28 March 2011.

BI060, Dhofar Veterans Panel. Interview by Interview by Mark Battjes, Ben Boardman, Robert Green, Richard Johnson, Aaron Kaufman, Dustin Mitchell, Nathan Springer, and Thomas Walton, 2 April 2011.

BI070, Retired General Officer. Interview by Interview by Mark Battjes, Ben Boardman, Robert Green, Richard Johnson, Aaron Kaufman, Dustin Mitchell, Nathan Springer, and Thomas Walton, 30 March 2011.

BI080, Retired General Officer. Interview by Ben Boardman, Robert Green, Nathan Springer, and Thomas Walton, 3 April 2011.

BI090, Retired General Officer. Interview by Ben Boardman, Robert Green, Nathan Springer, and Thomas Walton, 4 April 2011.

BI100, Senior Army Officer. Interview by Mark Battjes, Richard Johnson, Aaron Kaufman, and Dustin Mitchell, 4 April 2011.

BI110, Battalion Commander. Interview by Mark Battjes, Richard Johnson, and Dustin Mitchell, 8 April 2011.

BI120, Retired Army Officer. Interview by Ben Boardman, Robert Green, Nathan

Springer, and Thomas Walton, 8 April 2011.

BI130, Platoon Commander. Interview by Ben Boardman and Richard Johnson, 5 April 2011.

BI140, Afghan Army Adviser. Interview by Ben Boardman and Richard Johnson, 5 April 2011.

BI150, Company Sergeant Major. Interview by Aaron Kaufman and Dustin Mitchell, 5 April 2011.

BI160, Company 2nd In Command. Interview by Aaron Kaufman and Dustin Mitchell, 5 April 2011.

BI170, Afghan Army Adviser. Interview by Aaron Kaufman and Dustin Mitchell, 5 April 2011.

BI190, Senior Non-Commissioned Officer. Interview by Mark Battjes and Thomas Walton, 5 April 2011.

BI200, Platoon Commander. Interview by Aaron Kaufman and Dustin Mitchell, 7 April 2011.

BI210, Company 2nd In Command. Interview by Mark Battjes and Thomas Walton, 7 April 2011.

BI220, Field Grade Officer. Interview by Aaron Kaufman and Dustin Mitchell, 7 April 2011.

BI230, Company Commander. Interview by Robert Green and Nathan Springer, 7 April 2011.

BI240, Company Grade Officer. Interview by Benjamin Boardman and Richard Johnson, 7 April 2011.

BI250, Battalion Commander. Interview by Benjamin Boardman and Richard Johnson, 7 April 2011.

BI260, Non-Commissioned Officer. Interview by Robert Green and Nathan Springer, 7 April 2011.

BI270, Company Grade Officer. Interview by Mark Battjes and Thomas Walton, 7 April 2011.

BI280, Commander's Panel. Interview by Richard Johnson, 1 April 2011.

BI290, Battery Commander. Interview by Richard Johnson, 1 April 2011.

BI300, Company Commander. Interview by Richard Johnson, 2 April 2011.

BI310, Company Commander. Interview by Benjamin Boardman and Nathan Springer, 31 March 2011.

BI320, Field Grade Officer. Interview by Benjamin Boardman and Dustin Mitchell, 29 March 2011.

BI330, Dhofar Veteran. Interview by Robert Green, 28 March 2011.

Washington, DC

BH010, Senior Policy Official. Interview by Mark Battjes, Ben Boardman, Robert Green, Richard Johnson, Aaron Kaufman, Dustin Mitchell, Nathan Springer, and Thomas Walton, 21 March 2011.

BH020, Brigade Commander. Interview by Mark Battjes, Ben Boardman, Robert Green, Richard Johnson, Aaron Kaufman, Dustin Mitchell, Nathan Springer, and Thomas Walton, 21 March 2011.

BH030, Iraq Veterans Panel. Interview by Mark Battjes, Robert Green, Aaron Kaufman, and Dustin Mitchell, 22 March 2011.

BH040, Afghanistan Veterans Panel. Interview by Richard Johnson, Aaron Kaufman, Nathan Springer, and Thomas Walton, 24 March 2011.

BH050, Historian. Interview by Mark Battjes, Robert Green, Richard Johnson, Aaron Kaufman, and Dustin Mitchell, 22 March 2011.

BH060, Vietnam Political and Military Analyst. Interview by Mark Battjes, Ben Boardman, Robert Green, and Dustin Mitchell, 24 March 2011.

BH070, Iraqi Mayor. Interview by Mark Battjes and Robert Green, 25 March 2011.

<u>Official Reports and Memoranda</u>

Anti-Guerrilla Operations in Dhofar Lessons Learned

BATT Notes on Raising and Training of Irregular Forces in Dhofar, Annex B to Section 10 of unknown report, Middle East Centre, St. Anthony's College, Oxford, UK

British Army Tactical Doctrine Retrieval Cell. "CSAF Assessment in Dhofar." Oman: CSAF, 16 FEB 1972.

———. Dhofar presentations, Alanbrooke Hall, Staff College, UK, 30 June 1982.

Irregular Forces – SAF View, Annex A to Section 10 General Graham Papers, Middle East Centre, St. Anthony's College, Oxford, UK

<u>Personal Accounts</u>

Akehurst, John. *We Won a War, The Campaign in Oman 1965-1975*. Great Britain: Biddles Ltd., 1982

Chiarelli, Peter, and Patrick Michaelis. "The Requirements for Full-Spectrum Operations." *Military Review* (July-August 2005): 4-17.

Clutterbuck, Richard L. *The Long, Long War Counterinsurgency in Malaya and Vietnam.* New York: Frederick A. Praeger, 1966.

Collier, Craig. "Now That We're Leaving Iraq, What Did We Learn?" *Military Review* (September-October 2010): 88-93.

Franks, Tommy. *American Soldier.* New York: Harper Collins, 2004

Gardiner, Ian. *In the Service of the Sultan A First Hand Account of the Dhofar Insurgency.* South Yorkshire, England: Pen & Sword Books Limited, 2007

Jeapes, Tony. *SAS: Operation Oman.* London: William Kimber, 1980

———. *SAS: Secret War.* Surrey: Harper Collins, 1996

Komer, Robert. *Bureaucracy at War: U.S. Performance in the Vietnam Conflict.* Boulder, CO: Westview Press, 1986.

Perkins, Ken. *A Fortunate Soldier*, London: Brassey's Defence Publishers Limited, 1988

Ray, Bryan. *Dangerous Frontiers Campaigning in Somaliland and Oman.* South Yorkshire, England: Pen & Sword Books Limited, 2008

Sibley, Paul. *A Monk in the SAS*, London: Spiderwise Publishing, 2011

Smith, Neil and Sean MacFarland. "Anbar Awakens: The Tipping Point." *Military Review* (March-April 2008): 41-53.

<u>Documents</u>

Coalition Provisional Authority. "Order No. 1, De'Ba'athification of Iraqi Society." 16 May 2003.

———.Order No. 2, "Dissolution of Entities." 23 May 2003.

———."Regulation No. 1." 16 May 2003. http://www.iraqcoalition.org/regulations/ 20030516_CPAREG_1_The_Coalition_Provisional_Authority_.pdf (accessed 1 May 2011).

———."Order No. 7." 9 June 2003. http://www.iraqcoalition.org/regulations/20030610_CPAORD_7_Penal_Code.pdf (accessed 1 May 2011).

———. "Order No. 3, (Revised) (Amended)." 31 December 2003. http://www.iraqcoalition.org/regulations/20031231_CPAORD3_REV__AMD_.pdf (accessed 1 May 2011).

Iraqi Governing Council. "Transitional Administrative Law." 8 March 2004. http://www.constitution.org/cons/iraq/TAL.html (accessed 1 May 2011).

United Nations Security Council. "Resolution 1483." 22 May 2003. http://www.un.org/ Docs /sc/unsc_resolutions03.html (accessed 1 May 2011).

———. "Resolution 1511." 16 October 2003. http://www.un.org/Docs/sc/ unsc_resolutions03.html (accessed 1 May 2011).

———. "Resolution 1546." 8 June 2004. http://www.un.org/Docs/sc/ unsc_resolutions04.html (accessed 1 May 2011).

———. "Resolution 1637." 8 November 2005. http://www.un.org/Docs/sc/unsc_resolutions05.htm (accessed 1 May 2011).

———. "Resolution 1723." 28 November 2006. http://www.un.org/Docs/sc/unsc_resolutions06.htm (accessed 1 May 2011).

———. "Resolution 1790." 18 December 2007. http://www.un.org/Docs/sc/unsc_resolutions07.htm (accessed 1 May 2011).

Doctrinal References

Adjutant General's Office, U. S. War Department. *General Orders Number 100*, Washington, DC: War Department, 1863.

Army, Department of the. Field Manual 27-10, *The Law of Land Warfare*. Washington, DC: Department of the Army, 1956.

———. Field Manual 3-24, *Counterinsurgency.* Washington DC: Department of the Army, 2006.

———. Field Manual 1-02, *Operational Terms and Graphics*. Washington D.C.:Department of the Army, 2004.

Ministry of Defence. British Army Field Manual Volume 1 Part 10, *Countering Insurgency*. London: Ministry of Defense, 2010.

Training and Doctrine Command, TRADOC PAM 525-3-0, *The Army Capstone Concept: Operational Adaptability—Operating Under Conditions of Uncertainty and Complexity in an Era of Persistent Conflict* Fort Monroe, VA: Government Printing Office, 2009

Secondary Sources

Afsar, Shahid and Chris Samples. "The Taliban: An Organizational Analysis." *Military Review* (May-June 2008): 58-73.

Al-Jabouri, Najim Abed and Sterling Jensen. "The Iraqi and AQI Roles in the Sunni Awakening." *Prism* 2, no. 1 (2010): 3-18.

Andrade, Dale. "Westmoreland Was Right: Learning the Wrong Lessons from the Vietnam War." *Small Wars and Insurgencies* 19, No. 2 (June 2008): 145-181.

Baker, Jay B. "Tal Afar 2005: Laying the Counterinsurgency Framework." *Army*

(June 2009): 61-67.

Beckett, Ian. "The British Counter-insurgency Campaign in Dhofar, 1965-1975." In *Counterinsurgency in Modern Warfare*, edited by Marston, Daniel and Carter Malkasian, 175-190. Oxford: Osprey Publishing, 2010.

Bergerud, Eric. *The Dynamics of Defeat: The Vietnam War in Hau Nghia Province.* Boulder, CO: Westview Press, Inc., 1991.

Birtle, Andrew J. *U.S. Army Counterinsurgency and Contingency Operations Doctrine 1860-1941.* Washington, DC: Center of Military History, United States Army, 2003.

Burton, Brian and John Nagl. "Learning As We Go: The US Army Adapts to COIN in Iraq, July 2004-December 2006." *Small Wars and Insurgencies* 19, no. 3 (September 2008): 303-327.

Clausewitz, Carl von. *On War.* Edited and translated by Howard, Michael and Peter Paret. Princeton, NJ: Princeton University Press, 1976.

Cordesman, Anthony H. *Iraqi Security Forces, A Strategy for Success,* Connecticut: Praeger Security International, 2006.

Fontenot, Gregory, E. J. Degan, and David Tohn. *On Point, The United States Army in Operation IRAQI FREEDOM.* Fort Leavenworth, KS: Combat Studies Institute Press, 2004.

Galula, David. *Counterinsurgency Warfare: Theory and Practice.* Saint Petersburg, FL: Glenwood Press, 1964.

———. *Pacification in Algeria, 1956-1958.* Santa Monica, CA: Rand Corporation, 2006.

Gentile, Gian. "A Strategy of Tactics: Population Centric COIN and the Army." *Parameters* (Autumn 2009): 5-17.

Gordon, Michael R. and Bernard E. Trainor. *Cobra II.* New York: Pantheon Books, 2006.

Green, T.N. *The Guerilla: Selections from the Marine Corps Gazzette.* New York: Praeger, 2005.

Gywnn, Major General Sir Charles W. *Imperial Policing.* London: MacMillian and CO. Ltd., 1934.

Hoffman, Frank. "Neo-Classical Counter-Insurgency?" *Parameters,* Summer 2007: 77-87.

Howard, Michael. *Clausewitz: A Very Short Introduction.* Oxford: Oxford University Press, 2002.

Hunt, Richard. *Pacification: The American Struggle for Vietnam's Hearts and Minds.* Boulder, CO: Westview Press, 1995.

Iron, Richard. "Britain's Longest War: Northern Ireland 1967-2007." In *Counterinsurgency in Modern Warfare,* edited by Daniel Marston, and Carter Malkasian, 157-174. Oxford: Osprey Publishing, 2010.

Joes, Anthony James. "Counterinsurgency in the Philippines, 1898-1954." In *Counterinsurgency in Modern Warfare,* edited by Daniel Marston, and Carter Malkasian, 39-56. Oxford: Osprey Publishing, 2010.

Kilcullen, David. *Counterinsurgency.* New York:Oxford University Press, 2010

———. *The Accidental Guerrilla : Fighting Small Wars in the Midst of a Big One.* New York: Oxford University Press, 2009.

Kitson, Frank. *Low Intensity Operations: Subversion, Insurgency, Peacekeeping.*

London: Archon Books, 1971.

———. *Bunch of Five.* London: Faber and Faber, 1977.

Krepinevich, Andrew F. Jr. *The Army and Vietnam.* Baltimore, MD: Johns Hopkins University Press, 1986.

Linn, Brian. *The Philippine War, 1899-1902.* Lawrence, KS: University of Kansas Press, 2000.

Mackinlay, John. *The Insurgent Archipelago: From Mao to Bin Laden.* New York.: Columbia University Press, 2009.

Mackinlay, John and Alison Al-Baddawy. *Rethinking Counterinsurgency.* Santa Monica, CA: 2008.

Malkasian, Carter. "Counterinsurgency in Iraq." In *Counterinsurgency in Modern Warfare,* edited by Daniel Marston, and Carter Malkasian, 287-310. Oxford: Osprey Publishing, 2010.

———. "The Role of Perceptions and Political reform in Counterinsurgency: The Case of Western Iraq, 2004-2005." *Small Wars and Insurgencies* 17, no 3 (September 2006): 367-394.

Mansfield, Don. "The Irish Republican Army and Northern Ireland." In *Insurgency in the Modern World,* edited by O'Neill, Bard, 44-85. Boulder, CO: Westview Press, 1980.

Mao, Tse-Tung. *On Guerrilla Warfare.* New York: Praeger, 1961.

Markel, Wade. "Draining the Swamp: The British Strategy of Population Control." *Parameters* (Spring 2006): 35-48.

Marston, Daniel. "Adaptation in the Field: The British Army's Difficult Campaign in Iraq." *Security Challenges* 6, no. 1 (Autumn 2010): 71-84.

———. "Lost and Found in the Jungle." In *Big Wars and Small Wars,* edited by Hew Strachan, 96-114. London: Routledge, 2006.

———. "Realizing the Extent of Our Errors and Forging the Road Ahead: Afghanistan 2001-2010." In *Counterinsurgency in Modern Warfare,* edited by Marston, Daniel and Carter Malkasian, 251-286. Oxford: Osprey Publishing, 2010.

Marston, Daniel, and Carter Malkasian, eds. *Counterinsurgency in Modern Warfare.* Oxford: Osprey Publishing, 2008.

McCoy, Alfred W. *Policing America's Empire.* Madison, WI: The University of Wisconsin Press, 2009.

McCuen, John J. *The Art of Counter-Revolutionary War.* Harrisburg, PA: Stackpole Books, 1966.

McMaster, H. R. "Crack in the Foundation: Defense Transformation and the Underlying Assumption of Dominant Knowledge in Future War" Carlisle Barracks, Pennsylvania: Research Projects, U.S. Army War College, 2003

———."On War: Lessons to be Learned," *Survival: Global Politics and Strategy,* 50, no. 1 (2008)

Metz, Steven. "New Challenges and Old Concepts: Understanding the 21st Century Insurgency." *Parameters* (Winter 2007-2008): 20-32.

Miers, Richard. *Shoot to Kill.* London: Faber and Faber, 1959.

O'Neill, Bard. "Revolutionary War in Oman." In *Insurgency in the Modern World,* edited by O'Neill, Bard, 213-234. Boulder, CO: Westview Press, 1980.

O'Neill, Mark. *Confronting the Hydra.* Sydney, Australia: Lowy Institute, 2009.

Paget, Julian. *Counterinsurgency Operations*. New York: Walker and Company, 1967.

Paret, Peter. *French Revolutionary Warfare from Indochina to Algeria: The Analysis of a Political and Military Doctrine*. New York: Frederick A. Praeger, 1964.

Race, Jeffrey. *War Comes to Long An*. California: UC Press, 1972.

Ricks, Thomas E. *Fiasco, The American Military Adventure in Iraq*. New York: Penguin Group USA, 2007.

Rubin, Barnett and Ahmed Rashid. "The Great Game to the Great Bargain." *Foreign Affairs* 87, no. 6 (November-December 2008): 30-44.

Russel, James A. *Innovation, Transformation, and War: Counterinsurgency Operations in Anbar and Ninewah, Iraq, 2005-2007*. Stanford, CA: Stanford Security Studies, 2011.

Schadlow, Nadia. "War and the Art of Governance," *Parameters* Autumn 2003.

Semple, Michael and Fotini Christia. "How to Flip the Taliban." *Foreign Affairs* (July-August 2009).

Shy, John, and Thomas Collier. "Revolutionary war." In *Makers of Modern Strategy : Military Thought from Machiavelli to the Nuclear Age*, edited by Peter Paret, 815-862. Princeton, NJ: Princeton University Press., 1986.

Stubbs, Richard. "From Search and Destroy to Hearts and Minds: The Evolution of British Strategy in Malaya 1948-60." In *Counterinsurgency in Modern Warfare*, edited by Marston, Daniel and Carter Malkasian, 101-118. Oxford: Osprey Publishing, 2010.

Thompson, Robert. *Defeating Communist Insurgency*. London: Chatto and Windus, 1967.

Thompson, W. Scott and Donaldson Frizzell. *The Lessons of Vietnam*. New York: Crane, Russak and Company, 1977.

Thornton, Rod. "Getting It Wrong: The Crucial Mistakes Made in the Early Stages of the British Army's Deployment to Northern Ireland." *Journal of Strategic Studies* 30, no. 1 (February 2007): 73-107.

Trinquier, Roger. *Modern Warfare: A French View of Counterinsurgency*. Westport, Connecticut: Praego, 1964.

Ucko, David. *The New Counterinsurgency Era: Transforming the US Military for Modern Wars*. Washington DC: Georgetown University Press, 2009.

West, Bing. *The Strongest Tribe*. New York: Random House, 2009.

Wright, Donald P., and Timothy Reese. *On Point II*. Fort Leavenworth, KS: Combat Studies Institute, 2008.